# HAUNTED
## SPRINGFIELD,
## ILLINOIS

# HAUNTED
## SPRINGFIELD,
## ILLINOIS

### GARRET MOFFETT

Haunted
America

Published by Haunted America

A Division of The History Press

Charleston, SC 29403

www.historypress.net

Copyright © 2011 by Garret Moffett

All rights reserved

First published 2011

Manufactured in the United States

ISBN 978.1.60949.257.1

Library of Congress Cataloging-in-Publication Data

Moffett, Garret.

Haunted Springfield, Illinois / Garret Moffett.

p. cm.

ISBN 978-1-60949-257-1

1. Haunted places--Illinois--Springfield. I. Title.

BF1472.U6M6325 2011

133.109773'56--dc22

2011013460

*This book is dedicated to my high school sweetheart and wife, Monica.*

# CONTENTS

# ACKNOWLEDGEMENTS

My thanks to the Sangamon Valley Collection, the Abraham Lincoln Presidential Library, the Illinois State Preservation Agency, the National Park Service, the *State Journal Register*, New Salem State Park, Camp Butler National Cemetery, the Dana-Thomas House, the Inn at 835, the Hickox House, Springfield High School, the Springfield Ghost Society, Edwards Place, Dana Quinn and a whole lot of people who wish to remain anonymous, but you know your contribution.

# LINCOLN'S NEW SALEM

In 1825, near the bluffs overlooking the picturesque Sangamon River in what is now Menard County, a hamlet of log cabins began to develop as a community. New Salem was platted in 1829, and before long, it was a bustling little village situated on a long and narrow hilltop. Also in 1829, the legislature gave permission to dam up the Sangamon River. Common talk of riverboats coming up the Mississippi into the Illinois River and then the Sangamon River to the port of New Salem created hopes of commerce and prosperity. Once the dam was completed, a grist- and sawmill was constructed on top of the dam over the river. Before long, more people were settling in New Salem, and it was a lively village of three hundred people, with log cabins, barns, a school, a church, a carding mill, a post office, general stores, a blacksmith and other craftsmen and a stagecoach stop.

Residents were busy preparing for the impending riverboat commerce and the wealth many hoped would follow. James Rutledge converted his home into a tavern, which was not a place of drink but a place where weary travelers could get a meal and a warm bed for a price. William Clary opened a saloon, which was more of a grocery. Doc Allen set up his medical practice in his cabin. Denton Offutt opened a general store to meet the needs of the villagers and travelers on the trail and river. Josh Miller was the blacksmith. Henry Onstot was a cooper, who set up his shop and made wood shipping barrels. He was poised to make considerable money when the riverboats arrived. Goods and products such as flour, grain and rice were all shipped in wooden barrels.

The Kelso-Miller dogtrot-style cabin and the Miller blacksmith shop next door.

New Salem's most notable resident was Abraham Lincoln, who moved to New Salem in 1831, when he was just twenty-two years old. He would live here until 1837, when he next moved to Springfield. As the community grew and developed, so did Lincoln. He once referred to himself as an "aimless piece of driftwood," but here he worked as a merchant, postmaster and surveyor; he dabbled in politics and studied by candlelight at night to become a lawyer. Lincoln was so popular with the villagers that they unanimously elected him as captain of the militia. He considered this a great honor. Lincoln's raiders went off to fight Chief Black Hawk, and when they returned, Lincoln told tales of the fierce fighting. Though no one in the unit was killed, the casualties were high. Lincoln finally confessed that the unit was never called to actual battle, but the mosquitoes in the camp were intolerable!

Unfortunately, by 1837, the riverboats still had not arrived, and Lincoln left New Salem to pursue his law career in Springfield. Only one riverboat, called the *Talisman*, had made the journey successfully in 1832. The water levels had dropped, and it became apparent that the Sangamon was too narrow and shallow for the riverboats to navigate on a regular basis. Without riverboat commerce, New Salem just did not have enough economic base to perpetuate the village. As this reality set in, New Salem began to die off. After only twelve years of existence, New Salem became a ghost town—in more ways than one.

Mother Nature and time were not kind to New Salem; cabins and buildings aged and weathered, and vegetation took over everything in the abandoned village. Within a few years, New Salem was in ruins. And though in life the people were gone, in death perhaps there are some villagers who remain in New Salem, attached to the land that once symbolized a dream of prosperity.

An interesting aspect of the ghostly events that occur on New Salem Hill is that today the entire village is a reproduction. New cabins and other buildings were built on the original sites of the old cabins. This suggests that the haunted activity may not necessarily be attached to the cabins; instead, haunted events here may be part of the environment.

One might be tempted to think that Abraham Lincoln haunts New Salem, and there are some visitors who believe they've seen a spectral Lincoln strolling through the village. However, this is likely the result of imaginations doing overtime. Sightings of a bearded Lincoln with his trademark stovepipe hat are suspect, as the hat and beard didn't come about until many years after Lincoln left New Salem. However, tales of ghostly apparitions of villagers going about their business and haunting their old cabins have been told for years by park staff and visitors.

The ghost of Elizabeth Herndon, who died a tragic death, is said to still haunt the village. On the early morning of January 18, 1833, Rowan Herndon was cleaning his gun and getting ready to go hunting. Lincoln was helping out at the nearby Rutledge Tavern, doing a repair of sorts, but he needed a particular tool. He sent ten-year-old Nancy Rutledge over to Herndon's cabin to retrieve the needed tool. When she entered the cabin, Herndon was loading his rifle. Nancy was explaining to Elizabeth what she needed when suddenly the rifle accidentally discharged, shooting Elizabeth in the neck. The bullet hit an artery, and blood sprayed everywhere. In moments, Elizabeth was dead. In a panic, Nancy ran out of the cabin and back to the tavern to tell Lincoln and the other folks there what had happened. Though it was an accident, Rowan Herndon faced suspicion from some of the villagers. Devastated at the loss of his wife by his own hand, Herndon left New Salem.

Visitors to the park walking past the Herndon cabin have occasionally reported seeing the ghostly apparition of a woman in period homespun clothing standing in the doorway. One of the most notable sightings of Elizabeth involved a family walking through the park. The young girl pointed at the Herndon cabin and commented to her parents that she liked the dress the woman was wearing. Her parents looked over to the cabin and didn't see anyone standing there. The mother asked her daughter whom she was looking at, and the girl again pointed at the cabin and said the woman

The Herndon cabin, where Herndon accidentally shot and killed his wife.

right there in front of the cabin. The parents still saw no one, so the father walked over to the front door of the cabin and found that it was closed and locked. Later, they were told about the history of the cabin and the ghostly sightings there. The parents wondered if their daughter had seen the ghostly specter of Elizabeth Herndon.

Another well-known ghost story told by staff occurs at the cabin of Jack Kelso, who had an unusual cabin built in the dogtrot style—two opposing cabins separated by a common breezeway but joined by a single roof. Kelso had one cabin, and Josh Miller, the blacksmith, had the other. A couple casually walking through the park one evening noticed one of the costumed interpreters leaning against the front of the cabin. He looked as if he was from the pioneer days, but he had on a hat with a wide, soft brim covering his eyes that seemed unusual to them. His arms were folded, and his head was slightly tilted down. The way he was leaning back against the cabin demonstrated that he didn't have a care in the world. But there was something inviting about this character, so the couple decided to walk over to him and say hello. As they approached, the man lifted his head to acknowledge the couple and then faded into thin air right before their eyes! Both staff and visitors walking by the cabin have reported seeing the same man within the vicinity of the Kelso cabin. They usually report seeing the man for only a moment or two before he disappears from sight. Staff members say that Jack Kelso was reluctant to leave New Salem even though the village was clearly doomed, and he was one of the last to leave. They further boast that if anyone would be haunting New Salem, it sure would be Jack Kelso.

The cabin of Dr. Regnier is known for an apparition seen sitting in an invisible chair out front. People who have encountered this ghostly specter say that the man gets up from his invisible chair and takes a few steps, then just disappears from sight.

Some of the reenactors who volunteer at New Salem have said that it sometimes feels as if someone unseen is watching them. One volunteer told a story that on a slow day at the park, while working on her craft in the Dr. Miller cabin, she sensed she was being watched. The moment she looked up, she caught a glimpse of a man stepping away from the doorway. She thought it odd, as usually she could hear people walking up to the cabin, but this time she heard no one. She got up and looked out the door but saw no one around.

The Rutledge Tavern, where weary travelers could get a meal and bunk for the night.

Sightings of ghostly apparitions are not the only paranormal events occurring in the park; people have also had phantom experiences. Working inside the cabins, some volunteers claim to have heard the phantom sounds of someone going about his or her household chores—sounds of a broom sweeping, the shuffling of boots on the wood floors, the clank of dishes— but the most bewildering is the occasional muttering of inexplicable voices. Unable to discern what is being said, those hearing the chatter say it lasts for only a few moments. One volunteer spoke about standing next to an old well by herself when she clearly heard what could only be the sounds of someone with a wooden bucket retrieving water from the well. She was so unnerved by the encounter that she stepped away from the totally dry and filled-in well.

Today, over 180 years later, New Salem is still a truly mystical place. Once you step onto the grounds of the re-created old pioneer village, you'll find yourself in a different time. Volunteers are dressed in period 1830s attire, and many of them portray characters of the village. Amble through the village and time seems to just slip away. Allow plenty of time to visit New Salem, as you'll want to take your time. Early in the morning, when the village is still lazy, just waking up for the day, is the best time to visit. Fires crackle in the stone fireplaces, giving comfort against the morning chill; the forest is alive with songbirds and other creatures; the sound of the river echoes through the forest; and the smell of the clean country air offers the same spirit of New Salem that has brought people to this hilltop since 1825.

# ABRAHAM LINCOLN
# AND HIS FAREWELL

Abraham Lincoln is said to have believed in the supernatural world. Accounts by Lincoln himself tell us about many strange visions and foreboding dreams that he had throughout his life, and one dream in particular may have predicted his death. Stories of Lincoln's ghost posthumously wandering are known all over the world. His troubled soul is said to haunt the White House, his tomb site and even the very streets of Springfield. Local folklore claims that Lincoln walks the streets after midnight between the Old State Capitol and his Eighth Street home. There are two buildings that truly resonate with the spirit of Lincoln in the historic district—the Old State Capitol and his law office. However, the remaining law office site was Lincoln's second and third law office; his first and last office sites no longer survive.

The day before he left for Washington, Lincoln went down to the office to tie up loose ends with his partner, William Herndon. Upon arrival, Lincoln looked up at the "Lincoln and Herndon" sign swinging from its rusty hinges and asked Herndon to leave it up. In a low voice, he said, "Give our clients to understand that the election of a president makes no change in the firm of Lincoln and Herndon." The men went upstairs to conclude their business, and when finished, they descended the stairs to the street. Lincoln declared, "If I live, I'm coming back sometime, and we'll go on practicing like nothing ever happened." Lincoln explained that the sorrow at parting from his old friends was great and made greater by his irrepressible feeling that he would not come back alive.

"If I live." Already, Lincoln was haunted by the notion that he might not return to Springfield alive. Tragically, his fears would prove all-too justified. Herndon was troubled by this statement. He tried to argue with Lincoln, but they were interrupted by well-wishers as they reached the street. Lincoln clasped Herndon's hand warmly and disappeared down the street, never to return to his office again.

Lincoln's fatalist view surfaced again in his famous farewell speech, delivered at the Great Western Railroad Depot. On that cold, rainy February morning before a crowd of well-wishers, Lincoln said, "Now I leave not knowing when, or if ever I may return." Lincoln would return to Springfield and the Old State Capitol one more time, and that would be posthumously.

# THE OLD STATE CAPITOL

The Old State Capitol building was important to Lincoln long before he made a big name for himself politically. He picked up his pay warrants in the state auditor's office when serving in the Illinois legislature. He argued more than four hundred cases in front of the Illinois Supreme Court. And he could often be found long into the night, shooting the breeze with fellow attorneys or researching cases in the law library.

It was in this building that citizens of Springfield said farewell to Lincoln for the final time at the last of his twelve funerals. This funeral was especially poignant and heartbreaking. Lincoln wasn't just their fallen president; he was also their friend and neighbor. He had carried their children through town on his shoulders and greeted them on the streets as he passed on his way to work. On May 3, 1865, the entire dome of the capitol was sheathed in black, but the columns below and the festoons along the cornices of the building were done in twisted spirals of black and white cloth. Nearly every public building and most of the businesses downtown were draped in black mourning accoutrements.

The doors to the Old State Capitol were opened shortly after 10:00 a.m., and an immense throng of people poured in. Springfield's population at that time was 12,000 people, but an estimated 150,000 people had poured into town to pay their last respects. Only about 80,000 made it into the capitol. For twenty-four hours, they filed into the Old State Capitol, six abreast, braving the scorching hot day in their formal suits and dresses for the chance to take one final look at Lincoln's face. Hardly anyone cried

The State Capitol in mourning for Abraham Lincoln's funeral in Springfield, Illinois, on May 3 and 4, 1865.

A *Harper's Weekly* sketch of Lincoln's funeral inside the Hall of Representatives of the Illinois State Capitol.

over the coffin—most were too shocked by what they saw—but when they reached the street, they broke down, leaning on one another for support. At 10:00 a.m. the next day, May 4, the doors to the Hall of Representatives were closed, and the undertaker reverently cleaned Lincoln's face one last time before closing the casket. As veteran soldiers carried the casket out the front doors, a choir of 250 singers on the capitol steps burst into song, and twenty-one guns were fired. The casket was placed in an elaborate hearse, and the funeral procession set off for Oak Ridge Cemetery. Though his body was laid to rest, Lincoln's spirit will not rest. His coffin was opened five more times to verify his remains and moved about seventeen times for his protection. In life, Lincoln did have happier days at his home in Springfield before the war, but is his hometown now haunted by his ghost?

## The Home of the Lincoln Family

One evening at dusk, a guided tour group was walking through the Lincoln neighborhood park. They had made their way toward the end of the street, past the Lincoln home, when the guide noticed five people lagging behind at the intersection in front of the house. The guide was about to call out for them to catch up when all five of them suddenly turned and stepped away from something at the same time. They seemed to be anxious about something, so the guide walked back to the group to see what was going on. He found them clearly unnerved; all five of them were convinced they had heard a horse and carriage coming up the street behind them. They claimed to hear the horse's hooves hitting the muddy street, and even the jingle of the carriage was clear to them. It was so sudden and pronounced that they quickly turned to get out of its way and to have a look, but all they saw was an empty street. The phantom carriage has been encountered a few times by visitors to the neighborhood, but the pungent smell of phantom horses wafting through the neighborhood occurs with more frequency.

But is Lincoln's home haunted? It is generally thought that the Lincoln home is not haunted by Lincoln. But there is suspicion that the home may be haunted by Mary and possibly the boys. There has been an apparition seen in the kitchen and parlor areas of the home. The ghostly figure is seen only for a moment, and it appears to be only about five feet tall. Mary was five feet, four inches tall, and the kitchen and parlor are two rooms where Mary would have spent a fair amount of time. The question becomes: why would Mary be haunting the home?

Perhaps not all hauntings occur out of an untimely or tragic death or unresolved issues on the part of the deceased. Perhaps some hauntings occur out of a bond or love for a place. When Mary lived in this home, it was the best and happiest time of her life. Mary was very popular here in Springfield; she threw fantastic dinner parties that were well attended, and her husband was a rising political star. Though an almost four-year-old Eddie Lincoln died in this home in 1850, Tad and Willie were born and raised here, also making for cherished memories. From the very first day Mary arrived in the White House to the very last day of her life, her life was nothing more than a downhill spiral into despair. It would make sense that Mary's spirit would linger in her Springfield home, where she was happiest.

Staff members before the National Park Service was involved in the upkeep of the home occasionally spoke of the phantom pitter-patter of children's feet running up and down the upstairs hall accompanied by childlike giggles. On one occasion, a staff member opening up the house one morning

The Lincoln home draped in funeral bunting for the funeral of Abraham Lincoln, May 3, 1865.

believed he briefly saw a child's hands holding on to the upstairs railing. The rocking chair in the living room area was said to rock on its own—and it did, right before the eyes of visitors! However, the gentleman caught tugging on a fishing line tied to the chair no longer works at the home.

Lincoln was fascinated by his dreams and spent time trying to decipher and interpret them. Lincoln was very much a deep thinker and sought knowledge and wisdom even beyond his dreams and visions. Since boyhood, the young farm boy sensed there was a greater task for him, a divine providence that he was destined to do something great. Lincoln also believed God was trying to send him messages through his visions and dreams, so he spent considerable time discussing them with family and friends, seeking the hidden knowledge from God. One of his most disturbing dreams occurred in the Lincoln home on election night.

On the night Lincoln learned he won the election for the presidency of the United States, Springfield celebrated big time. Fireworks and cannon fire celebrations went on late into the night. It wasn't until the early hours of the morning that a tired and exhausted president-elect broke from the celebrations and retired to his home. When he made it home, he went to his bedroom and laid back on a couch. He could see a little round mirror sitting atop a bureau across the room and suddenly saw a strange vision in the mirror. Not sure what he was seeing, Lincoln no doubt tried to logically explain it away. He may have said something like, "Oh, my eyes are playing tricks on me. I'm exhausted, it's late and it's been an excitable day." But moments later, Lincoln looked back into the mirror. The vision reappeared, and this time it was quite clear what he was seeing. He could clearly see a silhouette image of two faces—his face, in fact—opposing each other nose to nose. But what struck Lincoln as odd was that one of the faces seemed to have a healthy skin color while the other one was pale and quite gray, like the color of death. Again, Lincoln tried to dismiss this very odd occurrence, and perhaps it was some time before he could doze off to sleep.

The next day, he told Mary about this bizarre vision, and she believed she knew what the image meant. She believed that the two faces represented Lincoln being elected to a first and second term as president. But the pale and gray image meant he would not survive his second term. This dark omen would haunt Lincoln throughout his entire presidency.

But Lincoln was not the only one in the Lincoln saga with precognitive abilities. Perhaps his fate was written well before his presidency.

In 1838, John Wilkes Booth was only six months old when his mother wrote a poem titled "The Mother's Vision" in response to a recurring dream.

It foreshadowed her son's fate:

> *Tiny, innocent white baby hand,*
> *What force, what power is at your command,*
> *For evil, or good? Be slow or be sure,*
> *Firm to resist, too pure to endure—*
> *My God, let me see what this hand shall do*
> *In the silent years we are attending to;*
> *In my hungering Love, I implore to know on this ghostly night*
> *Whether 'twill labour for wrong, or right,*
> *For—or against Thee?*

## SPIRITUALISM, THE LINCOLNS AND THE WHITE HOUSE

Throughout the 1850s and 1860s, Spiritualism emerged for the first time and was the new rage across the United States. It was well practiced by the social elite of Washington. By the 1860s, over two million people were practicing Spiritualism across the country, using psychics and mediums to contact the dead and to gain insight into the future.

Once settled in the White House, Mary was introduced to Cranston Laurie, a well-known Georgetown medium of the day, and she quickly embraced the spiritualist movement, attending a great number of séances in Washington and subsequently hosting at least eight known séances in the Red Room of the White House. (I dare say, she likely held more.) Lincoln attended two of those séances.

There is some evidence to suggest that Lincoln developed an interest in Spiritualism and the séances that had become social events across the nation. After all, it appears that Lincoln himself may have had a genuine gift of sight. In 1862, a trance medium named Nettie Coburn sat in the Red Room of the White House waiting for President Lincoln to enter. Mrs. Lincoln insisted that her husband bear witness to Nettie's most unusual gift. Granted, there were plenty of charlatans about using parlor tricks to take advantage of the Lincolns, but Miss Nettie's ability was impressive, and she had a solid reputation amongst the Washington elite.

When Miss Nettie came out of her trance, she found herself standing before Lincoln, who was sitting back in a chair with his arms folded. Several others in attendance were speechless. Miss Nettie, who had no recollection of what she said during her trances, was told she had been talking about the Emancipation Proclamation, which was not yet public knowledge. She seemed to know details that were known only to Lincoln and his cabinet members at best, and even if some of the information had leaked to the public, how could she know the fine details of the Emancipation? It just did not seem plausible to the president. She further informed the president that he must not abate the issue or delay its enforcement. She declared that it would be the crowning achievement of his life. Although much of Lincoln's cabinet was against the Emancipation, Miss Nettie nobly stated that Lincoln should "stand firm to his convictions and fearlessly perform the work and fulfill the mission for which he had been raised up by an overruling Providence."

Lincoln responded, "My child, you possess a very singular gift; but that it is of God no doubt. I thank you for coming here tonight. It is more important than any one present can understand."

During his White House years, Lincoln had numerous meetings with Miss Nettie to gain insight into matters at hand. She once advised the president to restore troop morale by visiting soldiers on the battlefront while avoiding the officers. In one of her trances, she even drew a battle plan on a map—a plan that was known only to Lincoln—and thus gave him confidence that he had devised a winning strategy. She helped Mary contact her deceased children, Eddie and Willie. And in the final meeting between Lincoln and Miss Nettie in April 1865, she even warned the president of the impending danger that was just days away.

Though Lincoln died in April 1865, Mary Lincoln would continue to practice spiritualism and consult mediums for years until her death.

In 1862, eleven-year-old Willie Lincoln had passed away at the White House. This death was very hard on the Lincolns, as Willie had become their favorite child. Mary's bereavement was so out of control that she was told if she could not collect herself, she would have to be sent to an asylum. She made claims that the ghostly apparition of Willie Lincoln appeared at the foot of her bed each night for several weeks and that some nights he would bring sweet Eddie, with his boyish smile, providing her comfort that her boys had crossed over into the light and were okay. Perhaps this is how Mary finally worked through her grief.

But Lincoln didn't fare much better. The grief-stricken president locked himself in his cabinet room for several days. When one of Lincoln's secretaries, Salmon Chase, came in to check on him, he found a melancholy Lincoln sitting behind a desk piled high with toys Willie had once played with. Lincoln said to Chase, "Do you ever find yourself talking with the dead? Ever since Willie's death, I catch myself involuntarily talking to him, as if he were here with me, and I feel that he is." Perhaps Lincoln wasn't seeing Willie's ghostly apparition; perhaps he was feeling the presence of his son. It's also thought that because Lincoln refused to let go of Willie's spirit, the boy's spirit lingered on in the White House.

Whereas stories about Lincoln's ghost in the Springfield home are virtually nonexistent, stories about Lincoln's ghost in the White House are common. White House staff, presidents, first ladies and even visiting dignitaries all have spoken of bizarre encounters in or near the Lincoln Bedroom, such as unexplained rapping on walls and doors around the room, shadowy figures and a presence believed to be Lincoln. Others claim they actually spotted his ghostly apparition.

Franklin D. Roosevelt and Dwight D. Eisenhower believed they could feel Lincoln's presence in the room we now refer to as the Lincoln Bedroom, Lincoln's cabinet room during the Civil War. Because of Lincoln's resounding presence in this room, both these presidents believed they drew inspiration from the goodness of Lincoln's spirit and were able to work through whatever issue was at hand. Eleanor Roosevelt, working at her desk late at night in the room, claimed she could feel Lincoln's presence watching over her shoulder.

First Lady Grace Coolidge claimed to have seen Lincoln's ghost on more than one occasion. She said that one day, while passing the Yellow Oval Room, she was startled to see Lincoln's apparition staring out a window in the direction of the Potomac with his hands clasped behind him. She felt he was deep in thought, perhaps gazing across the river at distant Civil War battlefields.

But Queen Wilhelmina of the Netherlands had an even more vivid haunting. While visiting the White House during World War II, she was awakened by an insistent knocking on the door. Thinking that something was the matter, she rushed to open it, only to find herself face to face with none other than Abraham Lincoln, who suddenly disappeared right before her eyes.

Winston Churchill is believed to have had not one but two encounters with Lincoln's ghost on two separate visits to the White House. On his first visit, Churchill was sitting on the edge of the Lincoln bed, the very bed where Willie Lincoln died. He was pulling on his boots, getting ready to go down for a state dinner, when he looked up and saw the apparition of Lincoln silently gliding across the floor. On the prime minister's second visit, he was winding down the evening with a hot bath, a cigar and a brandy all at the same time. Churchill climbed out of the bathtub, cigar in one hand and brandy in the other, and walked naked into the adjoining bedroom—only to see the ghost of Lincoln leaning against the fireplace mantel. Churchill, as quick witted as ever, quipped, "Good evening, Mr. President. You seem to have me at a disadvantage, sir!" And with that, Lincoln's apparition softly smiled and faded into thin air.

President Carter's young daughter Amy had a child's playful séance in the Lincoln Bedroom with a Ouija board. She believed she was actually conversing with the spirit voice of Lincoln. But the joke was on Amy. A Secret Service agent had placed a little microphone and speaker in the room that night and was having a little fun with the president's daughter.

Not long before Lincoln's assassination, the president had one more prophetic vision. He spoke about it to Mary and his friend and security officer Ward Hill Lamon, who later recounted the president's words:

> *About ten days ago, I retired late. I soon began to dream. There seemed to be a death-like stillness about me. Then I heard subdued sobs as if a number of people were weeping. I thought I left my bed and wandered downstairs. There the same pitiful sobbing broke the silence but the mourners were invisible. I went from room to room; no living person was in sight, but the same mournful sounds of distress met me as I passed along. It was light in all the rooms; every object was familiar to me, but where were all the people who were grieving as if their hearts would break? I was puzzled and alarmed. What could be the meaning of this? Determined to find a cause of a state of things so mysterious and shocking, I kept on until I arrived at the East Room, of which I entered. Before me was a catafalque, upon which rested a corpse wrapped in funeral vestments. Around it were stationed soldiers who were acting as guards; and there was a throng of people, some gazing mournfully upon the corpse whose face was covered, others weeping pitifully. Who is dead in the White House I asked of one of the soldiers? The President, was his answer, he was killed by an assassin. Then came a loud burst of grief from the crowd which awoke me from my dream. I slept no more that night; and although it was only a dream, I have been strangely annoyed by it ever since.*

On the day of Lincoln's assassination, he held a cabinet meeting about two o'clock that afternoon. At the onset of the meeting, he told the members with a grave face that soon there would be terrible news. When pressed for more details, he didn't say much else but then mentioned a dream he had the night before. He spoke about being on a mysterious ghost ship adrift at sea, unable to find any port of call to sail into. And according to Lincoln himself, this was a dream that had haunted the president the night before his son Eddie died. He had the same dream the night before Willie died and whenever the Union lost major Civil War battles. This time, it would be Lincoln's last prophetic dream, and this one most certainly came true. Indeed it did.

# THE LINCOLN SPECIAL

The Lincoln Special, the president's funeral train, departed Washington just seven days after his assassination. The train made twelve officials stops in major cities so a grieving nation could pay its respects. The train made stops in Baltimore, Harrisburg, Philadelphia, New York, Albany, Buffalo, Cleveland, Columbus, Indianapolis, Michigan City, Chicago and, finally, Springfield. The nine-car funeral train carried the coffins of Abraham and Willie Lincoln in the second-to-last rail car. About three hundred mourners were also on board.

In the designated cities, the Lincoln Special would stop. Lincoln's coffin would be placed on a horse-drawn hearse, and a grand funeral procession would make its way through town. All twelve of Lincoln's funerals were elaborate and unmatched to this day in this country. Lincoln's procession would make its way to a county or federal building, where he would lie in state for public viewing. At the Chicago and New York funerals, 500,000 people attempted to file past Lincoln's coffin in a twenty-four-hour period. That's 20,832 people per hour paying their respects. They would have filed past Lincoln's coffin in a wide column, 15 to 20 people abreast, and they would certainly not have been given any time to pause for reflection.

But in the countryside, where folks couldn't make it into the big cities for the funerals, they would stand vigil trackside throughout the day and night, waiting for the Lincoln Special to make its pass. An estimated one million people stood by the tracks waiting for the funeral train, making it the largest funeral in our nation's history. If they had to wait through the night, they would build bonfires on either side of the tracks, not only to keep themselves warm, but also to honor the president. One of the mourners on board the train commented that there were so many fires

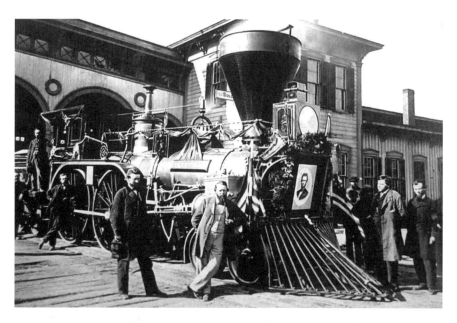

Old Nashville—one of several different locomotives that pulled the Lincoln Special.

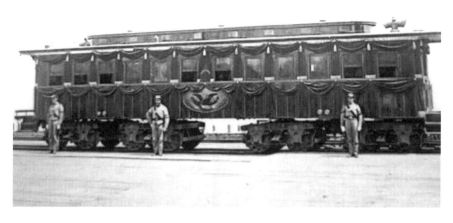

The funeral car that carried the coffins of Abraham and Willie Lincoln from Washington to Springfield.

lighting the night sky going through the state of New York that it was nothing short of an ominous twilight.

The Lincoln Special pulled into the Chicago-Alton Depot in Springfield, once located on the corner of Third and Washington Streets (the depot no longer survives) where the Amtrak station sits today, about 8:40 a.m. on May 3. Lincoln's coffin was taken to the Old State Capitol, and that's where the public had the final opportunity to look upon the face of Abraham Lincoln.

Today, some believe a ghostly Lincoln Special makes its fourteen-day journey from Washington to Springfield each year. Claims of sightings occur all along the old route where tracks still exist today, but sightings have even been reported in places where tracks no longer exist. Sightings tell of a ghostly pilot engine silently blazing down the tracks. Moments later, a ghostly funeral train silently blazes by. Other towns speak of the haunting sounds of an old steam whistle heard off in the distance on the anniversary of the train's passing through.

One of the earliest accounts of a ghost train comes out of Philadelphia just months after the Lincoln Special made its historic journey in 1865. A railroad watchman was out late one night in the country, walking the tracks with his lantern and looking for trouble spots. He could hear a faint steam whistle well off in the distance behind him. Turning around, he thought he saw the pinpoint light on the front of a locomotive miles down the track. He thought that was odd, as he knew there were no trains that time of night. But again, he heard the familiar whistle, and this time the light was suddenly many miles closer. He knew Lincoln's funeral train had come down these tracks just months ago, and he wondered if something otherworldly was about to happen. The man sat down in the grass next to the tracks and patiently waited. Moments later, a ghostly pilot engine came silently roaring by, followed by the nine-car funeral train. The glowing orange embers of fire and black smoke blazed out of the smokestack, and the breeze blew back the watchman's hair. As the ghostly funeral car carrying Lincoln's coffin went by, he saw Union soldiers standing guard around Lincoln's coffin. The tremendous event was over in seconds, and the watchman knew he had just encountered the ghostly Lincoln Special. Similar sightings have been occurring between Washington, D.C., and Springfield, Illinois, ever since.

Is the Lincoln Special making an annual journey? The Lincoln Special was the first of its kind; the nation had never before mourned a president in this fashion. Lincoln would instantly become a legend, and so would the Lincoln Special, still making its journey bringing the slain president's body home to Springfield each and every year.

# THE TOMB OF ABRAHAM LINCOLN

Lincoln's funeral procession entered the cemetery and stopped in front of the receiving vault. Lincoln's coffin was placed inside, the doors were closed and locked and sentries were posted to stand guard over the president. It was over at last for the martyred president—or was it? Lincoln's coffin would be opened five times and moved seventeen times before finding its final resting place.

Within two or three days of Lincoln's interment, mourners at the cemetery began to report sightings of Lincoln's ghostly apparition patrolling the hillside above where the tomb would later be built. This began to foster a superstitious belief that Lincoln must not be resting in peace, and some people began to believe he was not inside his coffin at all. Since his body has been seen posthumously wandering the hillside, he must still be looking for his final resting place.

Seven months after Lincoln was placed in the receiving vault, his coffin was moved up to the hillside crypt, freeing up the receiving vault for future interments. But perhaps spurred on by the claims of the president's ghost wandering the hillside, seven friends of Lincoln, who had entrusted themselves to protect the president, decided to open Lincoln's coffin for the first time and verify his remains. A plumber's assistant named Leon Hopkins went to the cemetery and cut out a small square opening in the top of Lincoln's lead-lined coffin. The men looked in. They saw Lincoln in the coffin, right where he was supposed to be.

In 1871, Lincoln's coffin was moved up to the tomb farther up the hill from the hillside crypt. The tomb was not yet complete, but it could receive Lincoln in Memorial Hall. Before encrypting Lincoln inside the tomb, those same friends of Lincoln decided to open Lincoln's coffin for the second time to again verify his remains. Keep in mind, the public still didn't believe his body was in the coffin. But again, Lincoln was right where he was supposed to be. Meanwhile, work on the tomb continued, but once Lincoln's coffin was inside the tomb, workmen began to report very strange things going on inside the tomb. The men spoke of phantom footsteps pacing the tiled floor, a doleful weeping echoing throughout the catacomb and a ghostly apparition of the late president wandering the tomb. The superstition that Lincoln continued to seek his final resting place was perpetuated.

By 1874, the tomb had been completed, and Lincoln's coffin was to be placed in a white marble sarcophagus, an aboveground burial crypt. The tomb would be opened to the public the following day. But before placing Lincoln's coffin into the sarcophagus, those same friends of Lincoln opened

The tomb of Abraham Lincoln and family. Abraham, Mary, Eddie, Willie and Tad are interred inside the tomb. However, Robert and his family are buried in Arlington National Cemetery.

Lincoln's coffin for the third time to verify his remains. Again, Lincoln was right where he should have been.

Now that the tomb was open to the public, people began to speak of similar ghostly encounters inside the tomb. Pacing footsteps were clearly heard, and the faint but doleful weeping caused a chill in anyone who heard it. The public also claimed to encounter Lincoln's ghostly specter walking the grounds surrounding the tomb, perpetuating the belief that he was still searching for his final resting place.

However, one of the real fears of the day was that someone might steal or desecrate the president's body; after all, there were still plenty of

The horse-drawn hearse lent to Springfield by St. Louis for Lincoln's final funeral. Springfield did not have a fancy hearse suitable for the president's funeral.

Confederate sympathizers around. In 1876, this fear came to fruition. A band of counterfeiters—not thieves, per se—made an attempt to steal the president's body and hold it for ransom. Apparently, they couldn't make fake money worth a darn. These men had Lincoln's coffin only a foot or so out of the sarcophagus when they were busted by the Secret Service agents and Pinkerton detectives who had infiltrated the gang. After a sensational shootout that began in the doorway of the tomb, a heated gun battle ensued. But things got a little confusing. The Pinkertons started shooting at the Secret Service, and the Secret Service started shooting back at the Pinkertons. The men escaped but were all captured about ten days later. All were convicted, but they were only given one-year sentences in the Joliet State Penitentiary. There was nothing illegal about stealing corpses out of a cemetery in 1876. They got that year in prison for destruction of state property—cutting the padlock off the back door of the tomb!

But was Lincoln's coffin returned to that sarcophagus? It was not; the sarcophagus had been damaged. Under the cover of night, John Powers, the curator of the tomb, and one of the marble workers moved Lincoln's coffin into a back labyrinth and began to dig a new grave. As the two men dug through the night, the walls of the grave kept collapsing because of water seeping in.

They were not about to bury the president in an undignified grave, but time was quickly running out; dawn was approaching, and the public would be showing up to pay their respects. These men could not be caught moving the president's coffin—it would be scandalous! So they gave up and simply covered President Lincoln's coffin with a pile of boards and debris left over from the construction of the tomb. For the next couple of years, mourners paid their respects to a memorial. Lincoln was not where he was supposed to be.

A year later, in the summer of 1877, Lincoln's coffin was finally pulled out from under the pile of boards and rubble. Work on the tomb's statues forced Powers to move Lincoln, but thanks to the workers, the public was made aware that Lincoln was not in his proper grave. The scandal rocked the town. This again fueled belief that Lincoln was not in his coffin. This time, his coffin was reburied in a shallow grave in another part of the tomb.

In July 1882, Mary Lincoln passed away. After her funeral was over at the tomb site, Robert wanted his mother hidden away with his father. Once again in secrecy and under the cover of night, John Powers enlisted the help of the friends of Lincoln, and together they took Mary's coffin into the same back labyrinth where Lincoln lay in a shallow grave. But the men had a late start and had used up a lot of time digging and moving Mary's five-hundred-pound coffin. Dawn was quickly approaching. They had just enough time to dig a very shallow grave like Lincoln's. No matter, as both coffins would soon have to have been disinterred while repairs were made to the cracking tomb.

By 1886, the repairs had been made, and the new crypt was in place, ready to receive the Lincolns for their final burial. But before placing Lincoln in the crypt, those same friends of Lincoln opened his coffin for the fourth time to verify that the former president was inside. Once again, Lincoln was where he was supposed to be. The Lincolns were both interred in the new crypt. This was to be their final burial, but in 1899, something catastrophic happened. The tomb had settled unevenly and had cracked from top to bottom. The government had no choice but to tear down the entire tomb and rebuild it. A mass grave was dug near the tomb site where the flagpole stands today, and the entire Lincoln family was placed inside. As the tomb was torn down, all the rubble was placed over the mass grave, protecting the Lincolns from any would-be grave robbers.

By 1901, the repairs had been made, and the tomb we know today was ready to receive the Lincolns' truly final burial. But there is one last problem.

Robert was still terrified and paranoid about another attempt to steal his father's remains. He had his mother and brothers safely tucked away in the wall crypts, but he demanded that his father be buried in a ten-foot grave

The reinterment of Abraham Lincoln and family back into the tomb in 1901.

lined with a steel cage. After his father's coffin was lowered into the grave, he wanted concrete poured into the grave, encasing his father in a crypt of concrete. Considering the permanency of this kind of burial, those same friends of Lincoln, who now called themselves the Lincoln Guard of Honor, insisted on opening Lincoln's coffin one final time.

These men placed Lincoln's coffin on sawhorses inside the dimly lit tomb. They also included some of their sons in the ritual—to "pass on the torch." They lifted away the small square opening one final time and were immediately overwhelmed by the sweet stench of rotting corpse. As they peered down into the coffin, the only notable deterioration was that Lincoln's skin had fully darkened and his eyebrows had fallen away. They noticed that the headrest of the coffin had deteriorated, and Lincoln's head was now tilted back. The men were greeted by the tuft of Lincoln's beard pointed straight up at them. They were all amazed at how well Lincoln had been preserved over the last thirty-six years; he was still recognizable. However, much to their sorrow, the American flag clutched in his lifeless hands was now faded, shredded and in tatters. Lincoln was lowered into his new crypt, and the concrete was poured over him, encasing him for all ages.

# THE FATEFUL DONNER PARTY

S pringfield is best known for Abraham Lincoln and its unique pioneer history, but there is a faded, yet bizarre, story associated with Springfield that is known today as the "Fateful Donner Party of 1846." It is a story that exemplifies *the* ultimate act of survival, one that is difficult for any one of us to comprehend in today's world. Though it is not a typical ghost story in the paranormal sense, there is no doubt that the survivors were haunted every day for the rest of their lives. Haunted by the memories of what they endured that winter of 1846.

California and the Oregon region were new and unsettled lands to Americans in the 1840s. Those tempted by the abundant land, bountiful game and the opportunity to own their land joined pioneer wagon trains headed westward. The pilgrimage itself was to cleanse the past; to settle in a new land and start a new life had become the American dream. It was attainable for anyone willing to take on the challenge and danger of Mother Nature and make the treacherous journey across an unforgiving land, across vast plains and a looming mountain range. Nineteen years before President Lincoln's death, on April 15, 1846, George Donner and James Reed, along with their families, several other families and hired hands, totaling thirty-three people on board a dozen wagons pulled by oxen, departed from Springfield, Illinois, from what is now known as the Old State Capitol Plaza.

Westward bound, the Donners' wagon train joined up with other wagons also headed west, and the main wagon train soon grew to nearly two hundred people and several dozen wagons. They followed the California Trail until they reached the Little Sandy River in Wyoming and set up camp. At this point, the migrants became divided over which trail to proceed on. Some wanted to travel the northern route through the mountain passes. It would take longer, but it was a known route and considered safe enough. Others, believing the supplies might not hold out on the longer route, were vying for a shorter but lesser-known southern route through the mountains. Overshadowing their decision was the fact that supplies were in fact already low, and winter would be arriving soon. Regardless of which route they chose, the migrants had to make it through the mountain passes before winter set in or they would risk getting trapped there by snow.

Complicating matters for those wanting to take the shorter route, they would have to catch up with Landsford Hastings, who was just ahead of them, guiding his own wagon train. He knew the shorter route, and George Donner argued that they could make haste and catch Hastings. There would be safety in numbers crossing through the mountains and reaching their destination before all the supplies ran out.

However, unable to agree on which route to take, the group split into two separate wagon trains. One wagon train headed for the northern, but longer, route, and the remaining eighty people making up the Donner party set out to catch up with Landsford Hastings.

As the Donner party trudged along, the wagon train was belabored by problems and setbacks, causing significant delays. The trail was barely passable in places; wagons had mechanical problems and accidents, and hills were steep, making it difficult for the oxen to pull the heavy-laden wagons. By now, they had traveled one thousand miles and were not far from their final destination. They had endured great hardship along the trail, but their greatest test and worst fears were yet to come. When they finally reached the Sierra Nevada Mountains at the end of October, they had to face the harsh reality that the so-called shorter route had taken them three weeks longer than expected. The Hastings wagons had already left their base camp and were headed through the mountains. They could wait no longer for the Donner party to arrive; Hastings had to get his wagon train through the mountains before winter set in.

Supplies were now dangerously low, and the Donner migrants were demoralized. To set up a winter camp where they would be forced to live off the land could mean starvation. The supplies would quickly run out, and adding to their frustration was the fact that they were now within one

A sketch depicting the harsh, brutal and unforgiving conditions that the fateful Donner party faced once the winter's snow arrived, trapping the settlers in the mountains.

hundred miles of Sutter's Fort on the other side of the mountains, where shelter and supplies would be available to them.

Because of the three-week delay, the only real choice was to push on and get through the mountain passes before the snow arrived. If they failed, it would mean certain death.

The Donner party pressed forward through the mountains, but the travelers were greeted by an early winter storm that blocked the mountain pass ahead. This would be the death knell for the Donner party.

Now the grim reality of having to survive a winter trapped in the mountains was becoming apparent. Pushing on through the snow-filled mountain passes was impossible. They had to suspect at this point that many of them would not survive. The migrants decided to hunker down and dig in for the winter, as it seemed to be the best hope for survival. They set camp at a lake now called Donner Lake, but survival instincts kicked in, and some of them wanted to push forward rather than face certain death. One-third of the wagons and migrants push on, but they made it only some six miles down the snow-covered trail before they realized their efforts were futile. The snow was too deep to walk through, let alone for oxen to pull heavy wagons through, and they set camp at Adler Creek.

Migrants at both camps could build only crude cabins that were really more like lean-tos. It takes considerable time and effort to build a proper cabin that will endure Mother Nature. They had few supplies to work with, and the snow was deep, making it difficult to cut and move heavy timbers. The winter's bitter cold made spending much time out in the elements difficult with the limited clothing they possessed. Furthermore, they were demoralized, and teamwork seemed impossible. Instead of banding together in a large group for survival, they huddled together in small groups, seemingly concerned only with their own survival.

By now it was mid-December, and spring was still just over three months away. With the food all gone, the settlers had no choice but to slaughter the oxen that had pulled their wagons; still, it would not be enough food to feed so many for very long. By now, all the wildlife had hibernated for the winter, and the migrants knew they would face a horrific death by starvation if they could not obtain food.

A band of fifteen men led by James Reed decided to attempt the less-than-one-hundred-mile hike on makeshift snowshoes to Sutter's Fort to get help for the trapped migrants. The survival of the starving camp depended on the success of their arduous journey through the deep mountain snow. The trapped migrants called these men the "Forlorn Hope," as their chances of reaching Sutter's Fort alive were pitiful. Yet without their success, there would be only one remaining survival option for the starving migrants: cannibalizing the dead.

On the treacherous hike through the winter elements, one man gave out and had to be left behind, certain to die of exposure. The fourteen remaining members of the Forlorn Hope soon became lost in the mountains, and they ran out of food. Starving, cold and caught in a raging blizzard without shelter, four more men quickly succumbed to the elements and died. It would be impossible to continue on without food, and there was no point in turning back. The remaining ten men had no choice but to eat the frozen and raw flesh of the four dead men in order to survive and continue on. Three more soon died, and their bodies were cannibalized as well. Barely alive, the surviving seven men of the Forlorn Hope finally arrived at Sutter's Fort, now Sacramento, on the western side of the mountains on January 18, 1847.

Between February and April, four different rescue parties set out from Sutter's Fort to rescue the trapped and starving migrants. When the first rescue party arrived at the lake camp, they found fourteen dead migrants and the remaining twenty extremely weak. They had been surviving by eating the last of the boiled ox hide.

The second rescue party arrived a week later at the creek-side encampment, where the rescuers were horrified to find the skeletal remains of the dead in some of the crude cabins. Their bodies had been cannibalized by the seventeen surviving migrants, now rescued.

The third rescue party returned with only four migrants, and by the time the fourth rescue party arrived, only one man remained alive. The last surviving Donner party member arrived at Sutter's Fort on April 29, 1847, just over one year from the start of their westward journey from Springfield.

Of the original eighty members of the Donner party, forty-four had survived by eating the flesh of the thirty-six dead. They would live on, but any hardships they faced as they aged would be nothing compared to their harrowing experience in the mountains.

Unfortunately, as if their personal demons weren't enough, the survivors had to endure years of criticism by the public. They were accused of murder and inhumane conduct, though no formal charges were ever brought forth.

George Donner and his wife did not survive, though all of their children did. James Reed's family was one of two families that did not suffer any losses, but it was James Reed who took the blame for the demise of the Donner party.

Today, the campsites at Donner Lake and Adler Creek are National Historic Landmarks.

The story is horrifying to tell, but to live through it is even harder for us to comprehend. Imagine these migrants trapped in the snowy mountains, living in crude makeshift shelters with no real food for months. When the last of the food was gone, the only option for survival was to turn to the bodies of the dead.

Imagine yourself outside in winter for months, with no food for days; you become weak and lethargic. Still, you have no food. Your body burns your muscles for energy, and you further weaken. Your stomach cramps into knots, screaming for any kind of nutrition. You curl into fetal position, hoping the cramps will go away, but to no avail. Days go on, and still no food. You beg God for food or death. You begin trying to eat frozen dirt, tree bark, even rocks—anything for a sense of fullness to make the cramps go away. Now delirium begins to set in, and at this point insanity begins to take over. Or perhaps you have just enough sense left in your mind to eat the flesh of the dead to live.

Eliza Donner later wrote in her diary:

> It had been snowing for three days, darkness came and somehow they managed to light a fire. They had been three days without food of any kind and most of them were far gone. Even in their delirium they knew they were dying.
>
> Even the wind seemed to hold its breath as the suggestion was made that were one to die, the rest might live. Then the suggestion was made that lots be cast and whoever drew the longest slip should be the sacrifice. The slips of paper were prepared and Patrick Dolan drew the fatal slip. No one had the heart to kill him.
>
> About 11:00 o'clock, the storm increased to a perfect tornado and in an instant blew away every spark of fire. The company was now engaged in imploring God for mercy and relief. That night's bitter cries, anguish and despair never can be forgotten. Somehow William Eddy got his dying companions to sit together in a ring and pulled blankets over them. A canopy of snow quickly covered the starving group. Antonio, a Mexican teamster, died. Franklin Graves was next. He died in the arms of his daughters Mary and Sarah. Patrick Dolan went insane and had to be held down by his companions. At last he slipped into a coma and died. Twelve-year-old Lem Murphy lay shuddering, all but dead. It stopped snowing. William Eddy crawled out of the white tomb where the dead and dying emigrants lay and managed to relight the fire. Someone cut the flesh from the arms and legs of Patrick Dolan. They roasted the meat and ate it, averting their faces from each other and weeping. The remaining flesh was butchered, wrapped, and carefully labeled so that no one had to eat their kin. Three days later the food was gone and talk of murdering for food became talk in the camp. We looked at each other with suspicion and we withdrew from each other. It was no longer helping each other to survive, it was now only the strong to survive. We were all going insane.

# SPRINGFIELD'S DR. FRANKENSTEIN

Mary Shelley published her novel *Frankenstein* in 1819 and introduced the concept of reanimation of dead tissue to the world. Just seven years later, in 1826, ten years before Lincoln arrived in town, a Springfield doctor would attempt that very same macabre medical experiment—sort of.

On November 26, 1826, the first of seven public executions in Sangamon County took place. A local blacksmith named Nathaniel Van Noy had killed his wife "in a fit of drunken rage" on the morning of August 27, 1826. He was indicted by a grand jury that afternoon, and his trial began the very next day. Van Noy was found guilty, and his sentencing took place on August 29, just two days after he murdered his wife. The judge sentenced Van Noy to the gallows, to be hanged by the neck until dead, dead, dead.

The gallows were once located at a little hollow on what is now the south side of the state capitol. (The state capitol was still in Vandalia at the time.) But these weren't the typical tall gallows on a platform with a trapdoor. The gallows here were simply two posts in the ground and another post connecting the two posts at the top with the hangman's rope dangling in the breeze.

But for as swift as justice was in those pioneer days, Van Noy would wait in a six- by ten-foot cell for three months for his appointment with the hangman. What Springfield had for a county jail was not much more than a rudimentary log cabin with only two cells, one for criminals and the other for debtors. The jail was affixed to the market building in the middle of the old city market, which was once located on Sixth Street between

Washington and Jefferson Streets. And just across the street on the corner of today's Sixth and Washington Streets was a whipping post used by the local magistrate at his discretion.

Van Noy's execution day finally arrived. Executions had long been public affairs, and the first one in Sangamon County would be no exception. Public executions were considered not only a form of entertainment, but they were also edifying for anyone in the crowd considering any wrongdoing. Historical accounts say that people poured into town from other communities, and thousands of people came out for the hanging. People lined the streets of Springfield to watch Van Noy, chained down in the back of a wagon, take his ride to the gallows. The death procession made its way from the jail down Jefferson to First Street and turned south toward the hollow. A number of other wagons filled with gawkers followed behind. The entire way, Van Noy led the crowd in singing hymns and reciting scripture.

Once at the gallows, the wagon was driven right between the two upright posts. Van Noy was directly faced with the rope. Thousands of people were gathered around the gallows, and most had never before seen a man hanged to death. The charges were ceremoniously read aloud to the crowd. A hood was then placed over Van Noy's head, followed by a noose tightened around his neck. The signal was given, and the wagon pulled forward, leaving its cargo dangling behind. Moments later, Nathaniel Van Noy was dead.

With a fresh corpse, all that was needed was a mad scientist. That scientist would be Dr. Filleo, summoned to the jail by Van Noy on the morning of his execution. Van Noy asked the doctor if a man could be brought back to life after he had been hanged. Dr. Filleo's response was that if the neck was not dislocated, and if he did not hang too long, there was a chance he could be brought back to life using galvanic batteries, which were nothing more than crude, low-voltage batteries.

Van Noy told the doctor that if he could bring him back to life, he would be compensated well. If the doctor was unsuccessful, then he could have Van Noy's body for medical dissection.

Before leaving Van Noy's jail cell, the doctor told him to lean forward and tip his head just before hanging to avoid breaking his neck. He followed the doctor's advice, and Van Noy's neck did not break. But the sheriff, sensing something was up between Van Noy and the doctor, ordered that Van Noy hang for a full hour, just to make sure he did not cheat the hangman. If Van Noy's neck did not break, then he no doubt would choke to death over the hour.

Finally, Van Noy's body was taken down and given to Dr. Filleo, who took the body to his office on Jefferson, between Second and Third Streets. There, the doctor affixed the electrodes from the batteries to Van Noy's lifeless body and attempted to being him back to life. Suddenly, the dead man's nerves began to twitch and spasm. But was it life? Repeated efforts by the doctor only produced muscle twitch after twitch. Van Noy was dead.

But the good doctor prevailed, no matter the outcome. If he had succeeded in bringing the dead man back to life, he would have been paid, and no doubt both would have become quite famous. Instead, he had a fresh corpse for dissection, and a fresh corpse was not always easy to come by.

Dr. Filleo wasted no time, and he began the dissection of Nathaniel Van Noy in his front office, with the door and windows wide open for all to see. In no time, a crowd of thrill-seekers gathered and packed around the windows and door to watch the doctor engage in his anatomical research.

It didn't take long for the crowd members to lose their enthusiasm for the spectacle of dissection, and people were now voicing their disgust at the degradation of Van Noy's body. But it was a medical dissection, and the doctor, undeterred by the crowds' comments, simply moved the body to the back room and continued.

It's not known if Dr. Filleo ever read *Frankenstein*. But the concept of using electricity to restore life eventually became a reality with medical technology called defibrillation, made famous by firefighter/paramedics John Gage and Roy DeSoto in the 1970s hit television show *Emergency 51*.

# THE CIVIL WAR AND CAMP BUTLER

If there is one place in Springfield where the dead speak, it would be Camp Butler National Cemetery. The tales these soldiers could tell would be beyond amazing. The fifty-three-acre national cemetery contains the graves of over twenty thousand of our nation's soldiers since the Civil War, and today it is on the National Register of Historic Places.

There are Union and Confederate soldiers buried here, along with soldiers from the Spanish-American War, World Wars I and II, Korea, Vietnam and the Middle East. There are even German and Korean POWs buried here who were relocated from a cemetery near Indianapolis. There are any number of notable interments here, such as Seaman John H. Catherwood, Medal of Honor recipient for heroism in the Philippine-American War; and the highest-ranking African American officer during World War I, Colonel Otis B. Duncan. Today, the greatest generation is dying off quickly, and most burials are now World War II veterans. The cemetery has recently undergone an impressive restoration project all too fitting and proper for our nation's honored dead.

As soon as the Confederates fired on Fort Sumter on April 12, 1861, President Lincoln called for fifty thousand volunteers to fight, and training camps would be needed to train the troops. The War Department sent General William Tecumseh Sherman, who would distinguish himself in the war, to Springfield to meet with Governor Richard Yates to decide on a location in Sangamon County for the new training camp. Sherman and Yates were not familiar with the county, so they took along Secretary of State Oziah M. Hatch and State Treasurer William Butler to show them the land. They selected an area a few miles northeast of town, between Springfield

The graves of the Confederate dead at Camp Butler National Cemetery, where Civil War camp life still plays out today.

and Riverton, called Jamestown (some called it Jimtown). Once the square mile and a half was secured by the secretary of state, the training camp was established on August 2, 1861, and named after William Butler.

Within a few days, the camp's first commandant, Colonel Pitcher, began to receive the first troops, and by the end of the month, there were five thousand new soldiers in camp. By October, the camp housed about twenty thousand soldiers.

Civilians answering Lincoln's call to service gathered at a schoolyard in Springfield and were put into ranks, and tens of thousands of new soldiers clumsily marched right down Washington Street through Springfield, past the statehouse (now the Old State Capitol), where Governor Yates and General Grant watched them head off to Camp Butler. There's an old legend that if you catch the wind just right at dusk in front of the old capitol, you can sometimes still hear the phantom footsteps of soldiers, the clank of gear and sergeants barking orders.

Just a few miles down the road to the east of Camp Butler is the town of Riverton. When the soldiers' training period was over, they would march from camp to Riverton. There, they would get on troop trains that would take them to Southern battlefields. Imagine being a young soldier who had just completed training, standing on a train station platform waiting for a train to take you to war. Waiting for that train must have been a defining moment for many of those soldiers. Emotions had to be high, and nerves had to be tested. Now, imagine how those soldiers felt when the troop train finally lumbered into the station. Reality must have set in at this point that death was a possibility.

It was no surprise to hear from people who believed they had encountered the ghostly apparitions of soldiers lurking around the old depot site in Riverton. But there is one figure seen in uniform leaning against a brick wall, apparently smoking. Other accounts claim that no one is seen, but phantom smoke can be smelled in the air.

In January 1862, Colonel Pitcairn Morrison took over command of Camp Butler. On February 16, Union troops captured fifteen thousand Confederates at the surrender of Fort Donelson, Tennessee. Six days later, two thousand of those prisoners were escorted into the camp. Though the camp was originally designed to be a muster-in point to the army and a training camp for soldiers, it was forced into service as a prisoner of war camp. Almost two months later, another one thousand Confederate prisoners arrived from captured Island No. 10 on the Mississippi. Prisoners from all eleven Southern states, except Florida, were kept in the camp.

The bivouac of the Union dead at Camp Butler National Cemetery, where old ghostly soldiers welcome other old soldiers into the brotherhood.

However, the camp stockade was not always so secure, and escapes were common. Camp conditions were deplorable. Illness such as malnutrition, dysentery, typhus and pneumonia decimated the prisoner population. Illness also ravaged the Union troops. Food rations for the prisoners weren't much more than hard biscuits and a cup of watered-down coffee. The hospital was always filled to capacity, and to have four or five deaths per day was not uncommon. The camp was ill equipped to handle so many prisoners; supplies were always low, medicine was almost nonexistent, the barracks were shoddy and the weather was harsh. Sanitation facilities were rudimentary. Conditions were so bad that, in an effort to slow the disease rate, a hospital was set up outside the campgrounds, away from the stockade of prisoners.

In June 1862, Major John G. Fonda replaced Colonel Morrison. The recruitment of soldiers was high by 1862, and camp was filled to capacity. Governor Yates was forced to open several temporary camps to handle the influx of soldiers. When Major Fonda was given the command of the 118th Illinois Infantry, a Colonel Lynch took over command of Camp

Butler. On July 17, 1862, a portion of Camp Butler was selected as one of the original sixteen national cemeteries designated by President Lincoln. Tragically, a smallpox epidemic killed seven hundred Confederate prisoners that same summer. Later, in January 1863, the camp received another sixteen hundred Confederate prisoners captured at Murfreesboro and Arkansas Point. Two months later, another five hundred prisoners arrived. The camp was still ill equipped and was not designed to handle so many prisoners; conditions were overcrowded. However, in May 1863, just over eighteen hundred Confederate prisoners were led out of camp on their way to Virginia for exchange.

Camp Butler's most distinguished service would be on May 3–4, 1865, when soldiers from the camp were assigned to function as a guard of honor for the funeral of Abraham Lincoln in Springfield. They were also assigned to stand guard over the receiving vault that held the remains of President Lincoln and his son Willie at Oak Ridge Cemetery.

Camp Butler was officially closed as an army training camp in 1866.

There are a total of 1,642 Civil War graves in the cemetery today—866 Confederate graves alongside the 776 graves of Union soldiers. The Union headstones are rounded at the top, in contrast to the pointed Confederate headstones. This distinguishing feature of the Confederate graves is said to keep the devil from sitting atop the tombstone, while others say, "It's so no damn Yankee will sit on my tombstone!" Some would say they are one and the same.

The Civil War still plays out at Camp Butler National Cemetery, with phantom sights and sounds of everyday camp life. Some folks living in the area of the old camp are hesitant to speak of ghostly matters, not wanting to be disrespectful to the soldiers buried in the cemetery. But they don't deny some of the strange things they've encountered over years.

Once in a while, especially in the summer around dusk, phantom smells permeate the night air, offering a haunting reminder of the camp's history. The smell of gunpowder is most frequent, says one resident, but another claims to smell the foul stench of disease wafting through the air. Both of them readily admit to, on occasion, smelling unseen campfires burning off in the distance. They even joke with each other, saying they hope the boys (soldiers) are warm tonight.

Soldiers from the old camp have made their presence known in other ways. Graveside services are not part of military protocol today. Instead, there is an outdoor chapel that is utilized for the cemetery service. Once the service is over and the family departs, the coffin is taken to the grave and interred. During one such military funeral, there were apparently several in attendance who believed they saw a Civil War soldier leaning against a tree about forty yards away, as if he were watching the funeral. He was seen for several moments, and no one saw him disappear, but when people looked back at the tree, he was gone. Initially, they all thought it was a Civil War reenactor in costume, but they later found out there were no reenactors in the cemetery that day. One witness described a grayish appearance to the man's uniform and his skin. However, he could not offer enough detail to determine whether he was a Union or Confederate soldier. These people found comfort in seeing this old ghostly soldier, believing that all of the soldiers in this cemetery are brothers sharing a common bond. This sighting was one old soldier welcoming another old soldier to the "bivouac of the dead."

When the camp finally closed in 1866, approximately 200,000 soldiers had passed through Camp Butler on their way to Southern battlefields. It was the second-largest camp in Illinois, next to Camp Douglas in Chicago.

But not all the ghostly activity in the old campground is related to the Civil War. My wife and I had an encounter with a World War II soldier that was absolutely amazing. It was a beautiful summer day, and we were driving through the cemetery and taking pictures. A military funeral had come into the cemetery to the outdoor chapel, and we stopped for a few moments to watch the military service from a respectable distance. After the service was over and the people began to disperse, we drove on. We reached the west side of the cemetery, and I saw a camera shot I wanted to get. My wife pulled the car over and parked. We could see over to the far northwest corner on the hill where there was clearly an open grave and a couple of guys standing around. A flatbed truck with a coffin in back pulled up. I commented that I thought the men would be burying the soldier from the funeral, and I got out to take a picture.

Several minutes later, I returned to the car, and my wife wryly asked, "Can the dead speak to you?" I told her that some people believed they could. She said that while I was away from the car, she heard a man's voice right outside her open window say out loud, "Nice day for a burial, isn't it?" She didn't see anyone, but she sheepishly replied, "Sure, I guess?" Looking around hoping to see the person whose voice she had clearly heard, she glanced into her side mirror and saw a crane lowering a casket into a freshly dug grave site. She thought to herself, "I wonder who's being buried" when again she heard the voice. "Don't worry, I'm not afraid. This is where I'm supposed to be." At this point, she realized it was the man being buried who was talking to her! Trying to maintain her composure, she quietly sat in the car, hoping I would return sooner rather than later. The man continued talking. "God Bless You," he said, and then, "John, John, John" (last name omitted). That's when I returned.

I immediately thought she was joking. "OK," I said, "I'll call your bluff. Let's go to the cemetery office and find out who was just buried." We drove to the office, and I went inside to make the inquiry while my wife stayed in the car. Office staff confirmed what my wife had said—the man's name was John. While inside, my wife noticed the flag flying at half staff over by the chapel and heard the now familiar voice of an elderly gentleman say, "That's for me, you know" in a laughing manner. She smiled and said to him, "Yes, I know."

# THE GIBSON GIRL HAUNTING
# OF LAWRENCE HOUSE

S pringfield socialite Susan Lawrence Dana inherited a good sum of money when her father died, and hoping to appease her father's spirit, she had an extravagant home designed and built by famed architect Frank Lloyd Wright. This could be Springfield's most credible and actively haunted home, and it's likely haunted by more than one spirit. This home can be highly creepy, even during the daytime home tour; staff and tourists report ghostly activity at all hours, day or night.

The history of this home is fascinating, and the life story of Susan Lawrence Dana is equally fascinating and quite complex. It is the story of life on Aristocracy Hill, one of privilege, world travel, wealth and social status but little happiness and plenty of tragedy. Two of her husbands died, and a third marriage ended in divorce. Both of her children died young; one lived only a few hours, and the second only two months. Susan was a Gibson girl of her time. Her eccentric lifestyle tested the boundaries of society, and she was a woman well ahead of her time. She kept her friends and the public guessing about what she might engage in next.

Upon completion of the home in 1904, Susan hosted a fantastic dinner party for all the workers who helped to build her new home. Subsequently, she began to play host to numbers of fantastic and lavish dinner parties that were well attended by other socialites. Susan continued to climb the social ladder in Springfield. She became known for her charitable nature and contributions to causes throughout the city. The house was built for entertaining, and entertain she did, receiving guests such as Governor Charles Deneen and John Philip Sousa.

The Dana-Thomas House, built by Frank Lloyd Wright. This is perhaps Springfield's most haunted house.

Spiritualism—consorting with the dead to gain insights into the future—was the new en vogue thing to do among the social elite. Likely at one of her dinner parties, a Spiritualist medium suggested that Susan write letters to those she wished to communicate with. The medium said wisdom would come with the responses. Wanting to appease her father's spirit, Susan wrote him a letter: "Papa, do you know all about the new home and are you pleased with it? Did I handle your will the way you wanted me to? I did the best I could. Susie."

She received a reply from her deceased father, but it's likely that the reply actually came from the so-called medium: "Susie I love the new house— Ed [her deceased first husband] and I often visit there together. You handled the will all right…Lovingly and devotedly— Father."

With so much strife in her life, Susan turned to the Spiritualist movement, perhaps seeking comfort and personal fulfillment. Between 1904 and 1905, she wrote several letters to her dearly departed and received ghostly replies from the other side. Susan Dana embraced the Spiritualist movement and became a practitioner herself.

In the letters, she appeared to be looking for insight into her financial future. Although she was an adult, she clearly still sought approval from her departed mother and father, signing her letters, "Your little girl, Susie" and asking if she was "on the right path." She also expressed great loneliness: "I am so lonely…my poor heart aches until I almost die…God help me I suffer so." The spirit replies were supportive, touting a higher mission in life for her and loving words of comfort, but they seldom gave any real predictions. Susan's letters and the replies were sometimes written on torn paper or envelopes. The handwriting was frequently sloppy and erratic.

Times were certainly good for Susan, but a series of family deaths caused her to withdraw from public life briefly. Susan found comfort and solace in her belief that there was more to life after death. She returned to throwing lavish parties but with a new twist. She began to now host numbers of séances in the barrel-vaulted room of the home, which quickly became the center of the Spiritualist movement in Springfield. Her occult parties were well attended, and she soon found herself as a Spiritualist leader in Springfield. She began to use her astrological name of Zane at her services and meetings.

She practiced her spiritual powers through things like slate writing, where the dead send messages in words randomly written on a slate by a medium, and speaking in tongues, where the living speak in lost languages. Susan's dead mother wrote a letter to Susan and instructed her to meet her in her old bedroom three times a week to receive wisdom and knowledge. Susan would sit and meditate in her mother's old bedroom, honing her medium skills.

Her séances and metaphysical meetings were well attended and soon outgrew the home. Susan moved the séances into one of her downtown properties, where her metaphysical society met with great attendance. The building still stands on Sixth Street above Cardologist and Springfield Novelties & Gifts.

Susan Dana and her cousin Flora lived in the house for a number of years, living the life of Riley—only with séances thrown into the mix of

The Gibson girl Susan Lawrence Dana in 1905.

social activity. Susan and Flora were close, and when Flora died, Susan no doubt felt very alone in the big home. She quickly moved into a nearby smaller home. In 1942, Susan was declared insane by a court of law and placed in St. John's Hospital, where she died four years later, in 1946. Her personal effects were sold off in 1943 to pay the mounting debt on the home, and her home was sold the next year.

Today, the well-preserved home is owned and operated by the State of Illinois. It is now host to a wide range of paranormal encounters that you would expect in a haunted home, but some of the paranormal experiences are inexplicably amazing.

During a Victorian recreation and reenactment of Susan's mother's funeral in the barrel vaulted room, the candles around the coffin kept blowing over, as if a strong breeze had materialized or someone deliberately blew on them during the service. Even the minister was distracted from his readings by the tipping flames, and people in the audience quietly pointed at the candles.

Motion alarms are occasionally tripped at night in various parts of the home. When staff members arrive to reset the alarm, they sometimes find that strange things have happened. One night, the alarm was tripped by a rainstorm, and a staff member went to reset the alarm. He stopped and paused for a moment, admiring the silence of the night broken only by the rain hitting the roof, when all of a sudden the fireplace grate started rattling and shaking for several seconds and then stopped. For him, it was time to go.

Another night when the alarm tripped, a staff member found things quite amiss in the library. All the curtains were off the windows and piled up in the middle of the floor, except one pair that was neatly folded over the back of a chair. The curtain rods were still affixed to the window trim, so in order to get the curtains off the rods, someone would have had to unscrew a number of brackets to slide the curtains off and then reattach all the rods and brackets.

Sometimes, when staff members arrive for work in the morning, they find things in the house askew. The home has perhaps one hundred doors between bedroom doors, closet doors and cabinet doors, and there are a number of tucked-away storage compartments with little doors. The doors are all kept closed for safety, fire and security reasons. One morning, an employee came in and was astonished to find every single door in the house standing wide open! Unnerved by such an encounter, the employee waited for others to arrive before going around the entire home in pairs, closing all the doors.

Another guide came in to work one morning and was in the basement when he heard someone come in the back kitchen door, which has its own separate alarm. Thinking that was unusual because it wasn't a door used very often, he went up to investigate. He found that he was still alone in the home, and the back kitchen door was wide open, but the alarm had not been tripped.

Strange things can happen right in front of staff and visitors to the home. The home tour begins with a brief slide show. One day, the guide was just about to start the projector when suddenly there was a loud crash elsewhere in the house. The guide went to investigate and found nothing out of place, but when he returned to the start room, the slide show had somehow started on its own. The slide was stuck on the last slide, having skipped the whole show. The last slide was a picture of Susan Lawrence Dana.

Objects that have been misplaced reappear moments or even days later without a plausible explanation. One employee was cutting ribbon and placing it across chairs so no one would sit in them. She set down the scissors and ribbon and walked away for a moment. When she returned, the scissors and ribbon were gone. No one else was around. A short while later, the ribbon was found on a chair, but the scissors were actually stuck into the back of the chair.

Visitors have seen a shadowy female figure breeze by doorways in the distance. When they ask their tour guide who the costumed guide is, they are told that guides are in costume only for certain events, not every day. Visitors also reported smelling cherry pipe tobacco in the butler's pantry on occasion. This was Susan's father's favorite tobacco flavor.

Unintelligible voices in low tones have been heard in various rooms. Some people claim to have heard heavy breathing. Even phantom music is heard playing from the musician's balcony, which seems to be a fairly active area.

Today, a particular dulcimer player has performed at the home for various events, especially for the home's Christmas open house. He has made claims that while playing one afternoon, the sun was streaming in the windows and was quite warm, but a sharp coldness came over the area at times, making it difficult to concentrate and play. A staff member once experienced a brief sharp cold breeze that gently blew through her hair. Another time, the musician's expensive high-end dulcimer suddenly lost tune while playing, which had never happened before. But the most bizarre encounter he had on the balcony came when a tour passed through with three stragglers, one of whom was in a long dark coat. She stood next to him and watched him play. He was playing "What Child Is This?" As he finished the song, he

Susan standing outside the south side door of her lavish mansion in 1910. The musician's balcony is inside the windows above her.

looked up, but she was gone—and there was nowhere for her to go without him seeing her. He broached the subject with a staff person, who said, "Oh, you've seen her, haven't you? She likes that song." Staff members speculate that it's the ghost of Susan's mother. Her ghostly apparition has been seen a number of times in the balcony area, and paranormal investigations have singled out this area as a hot spot.

Unnerving a number of people passing through the house is the sense of a presence felt when no one is seen. People feel that they're being watched. The house does have a creepy vibe to it, and people pick up on it even when nothing paranormal has been mentioned. But most unnerving for visitors and staff is the presence felt in the basement—and it's not nice.

The basement bowling alley is host to unexplained activity. Many people report feeling a dark and negative presence in the basement area, and many are unnerved enough that they're usually ready to finish their tour of the home. This negative vibe is heavy and some say palpable at times. One visitor claimed that his chest just started pounding and he felt panicky. He said he just "had to get out of there." An occasional inexplicable low moan has been audible to people and caught in voice recordings. Another recording picked up a low, whispery voice that said, "Go away."

Several years ago, before her death, famed psychic Greta Alexander toured Susan's old house. Once she was finished reading the house, she commented that the home was indeed haunted by a number of spirits, namely Susan, her cousin Flora and Susan's mother and father. But there is also a dark entity in the house that refuses to leave; it wants the house. Greta believed that during one of Susan's many séances in the house, this dark entity was unintentionally invoked. She further believed that Susan likely had trouble with this entity ever since. However, in death, Susan's, Flora's and Susan's parents' spirit energy all combined and are strong and powerful enough to suppress this entity and confine it to the basement, never allowing it to come to the upper floors of the home. Greta finished by saying that, entity or not, the Lawrence family would still be haunting the home because of their family bond and the affection they all had for the fantastic home that Susan built.

Today, the Dana-Thomas House is still alive with the dead.

# THE INN AT 835

Miss Bell Miller was born in 1870. She was one of Springfield's first professional businesswomen, starting her own floral business in the 1890s while only in her early twenties. Her florist shop catered to the wealthy residents of the Aristocracy Hill neighborhood of Springfield, and she became quite successful. Bell Miller's greenhouse once encompassed almost an entire city block, and by the turn of the century, Bell had become wealthy.

In 1909, she had Springfield's first modern apartment building constructed on the corner of Second and Canedy Streets. It was designed by the known architectural firm of Helmle and Helmle. The building contained six luxury apartments, including one for herself. The building was completed with several open balconies on each floor and large ornate fireplaces throughout, and the oak trim work was milled with impressive architectural detail. The building is on the National Register of Historic Places, and to this day, it retains most of its original architectural details and historic charm inside and out.

In 1994, a local businessman purchased the building, and each of the apartments was converted into a luxury guest room. It is now called the Inn at 835, Springfield's finest bed-and-breakfast accommodation. Each guestroom maintains the old historic charm, with luxurious accommodations such as private baths and Jacuzzis, and some have original working fireplaces and access to open balconies.

Legend has it that Bell Miller has never left her old home. She had a first-floor apartment on the south side, now a dining and reception area. Much of the haunted activity here seems to have resulted not from some tragic or untimely death, but perhaps out of love for or a bond with the place. Bell Miller's life accomplishments were astounding for a woman in her time, and her apartment building was the culmination of her success. Perhaps this is the reason her spirit remains in her old building today.

Bell was not only known for her charitable nature and kindness within the community, but she was also kind and sociable with her own tenants. She is said to have greeted guests and visitors to the apartment building with candy from a candy dish on the reception desk, and she socialized in a front parlor.

There have been numerous bizarre occurrences here, witnessed by employees and guests alike over many years. However, there are people who have been in the building for many years and deny any haunted activity. Nevertheless, if Bell Miller still haunts the place, she is still welcoming of visitors.

Bell has been gone since the 1940s, but today the sounds of a crystal lid being replaced on a candy dish can still be heard by new guests arriving at the inn, event though the lid to the candy dish has long been removed. One former apartment resident spoke of how tenants would come home and stop in the entry area to pick up mail or newspapers. On occasion, they thought they heard someone say hello, yet no one else was seen standing there. Some believe Bell still greets guests to this day with a garbled soft voice that says "hello there" or "welcome home." Bell's apparition has also been seen in the front entry and reception area. Witnesses describe her with hair pulled back, wearing a long-sleeved blouse and full-length skirt in a style unlike any fashion today. Most people seem to see her out of the corner of their eyes for just a second, but at least one couple believe they saw her at the front desk while they were coming in the front door of the inn. Others believe they have seen a womanly figure dart across the hall or through a doorway, startling them in various areas of the inn.

Some people believe they've encountered Bell's presence in the breakfast room. Others speak of similar sensations in the front parlor area. People relaxing in the wingback chairs sometimes sense that someone is watching them. Others claim to feel a woman's presence when a sudden inexplicable breeze flutters by. Employees are occasionally annoyed by a particular book in the parlor that seems to find its way onto the floor. Repeated efforts to reshelve the book are pointless, as it somehow finds its way back to the floor. Innkeepers say that it's like someone is seeking attention. Placing the book elsewhere or calling out "Enough!" seems to quell the attention-getting behavior for a while.

This is an original photograph taken during a haunted tour. Some believe they can see the ghostly apparition of Bell Miller standing on the landing inside the front door, where she is said to have once greeted visitors to the home.

Innkeepers occasionally deal with little pranks and nuisances that are mostly annoying. But there is one prank that is attributed to Bell that certainly got the attention of one of the innkeepers. One slow night, the front desk received a call from one of the rooms upstairs. The woman's voice sounded concerned; she said she couldn't get the thermostat to work and her room was cold. The innkeeper told the woman she'd be right up. But as she began to ascend the stairs, she suddenly stopped and recalled that that particular room was to be empty that night. She went back down the stairs and checked the registry; the room was, in fact, vacant. But the innkeeper was sure the call came from that room, so she went straight up to the room. She found the door closed and locked. It was inn policy to keep vacant room doors open. Concerned and equally perplexed, she knocked on the door, but no one answered. Using her passkey, the innkeeper entered the room and found the room empty. But she was suddenly taken back by the sharp coldness in the room; it was so cold that she could see her own breath in the air. Aware of a presence, she cautiously backed out of the room, locking the door behind her.

Then there is the strange activity of the elevator. Guests and innkeepers repeatedly claim that, regardless of which button they press, the elevator frequently stops on a different floor. Sometimes the innkeeper will have to

This is the only known picture of Miss Bell Miller.

call out, "Enough! Take me to the third floor." Innkeepers and guests have been known to give up on the elevator and take the stairs. The elevator doors have also been known to open by themselves when someone approaches the call button, just like at Springfield High School. Repeated maintenance and inspections calls on the elevator never reveal anything wrong.

But one of the more bizarre encounters involved a couple at the front desk speaking with the innkeeper and writing down some information on a small notepad. All of a sudden, the notepad went flying out of the woman's hand and landed on the floor several feet away. Perplexed, the three just looked at one another and shrugged it off. The woman picked up the notepad from the floor and continued to write—and then *swoosh*! The notepad went flying out of her hand again, as if some unseen hands had slapped it away. The innkeeper commented, "It must be the little boy" who runs around here. But are these pranks caused by Bell, or do they sound like the behavior of an attention-seeking little ghost boy? Some employees and guests who have had inexplicable encounters believe it feels like a young boy's presence to them.

Guests have occasionally reported strange activity during their stay at the inn. They sometimes share their stories in journals or notes left behind in the rooms for the next guest or the innkeeper. Stories from guests suggest they are more intrigued than frightened by their unexplained encounters. One couple who happened to be staying in the "cold" room on their anniversary had an unusual night. Late that night, while his wife was sleeping, the man was sitting in a wingback chair across the room reading a book by firelight. Thinking it odd that a chill overcame the room by the fireplace, he looked up and saw a shadowy figure in the bathroom doorway next to the bed where his wife was sleeping. In a second, it vanished right before his eyes. "It was really strange because I could see the moonlight shining through the doorway, but then it went dark, cold and dark." It happened in such a fleeting moment, he wasn't even sure it had happened and didn't give it much thought.

But several minutes later, the man, still reading in the chair, heard his sleeping wife say, "Quit it." He ignored her, but moments later she again muttered, "Quit it." This time, the man responded, and she told him to quit messing with her feet. He told her it wasn't him, as he was across the room in the chair. She sat right up in bed and claimed someone was tickling her feet. Neither claimed to be frightened by the night's events; they said if it was a ghost, it was just playing around.

Another couple staying in a different room spoke about sleeping one night when the man suddenly awoke to the sound of people talking in the room. Within a moment, the voices stopped, and the man thought maybe it had just been part of a dream. He went back to sleep. The next morning, the couple was getting dressed and ready for the day when the woman asked her husband whom he was talking to in the room last night. Apparently, she had heard the talking as well and had thought her husband was talking in his sleep.

For all the bizarre and ghostly activity at the inn, the antics are benign and harmless. Bell is still around, looking after her building, and she seems to enjoy the company of the guests at the charming old inn. The little boy is, well, just being a little boy. But there is also a mysterious third spirit that haunts the inn, and he may not be so nice. A tall, dark, shadowy man has made his ghostly appearance on a handful of occasions and has been caught on camera in the front door entry area. This mysterious shadow man has only been seen a few times, and he's only been encountered in the front foyer entry area, nowhere else in the inn. He always appears to be standing in a sort of arrogant pose and gives off a vibe of trespassing, as though he doesn't want people in his space.

Innkeepers working around the front desk area have, on a couple of occasions, looked down at the front door to see the shadow man standing there. One innkeeper leaving work late one night turned around as she walked to the parking lot and saw the shadow man standing on the sidewalk right in front of the front door. As you can imagine, she was relieved to be done with work for the night. She did not turn around for a second look. The man's identity and his reason for his presence at the inn remain unknown today.

Today, the Inn at 835 continues to function as the finest bed-and-breakfast accommodations and banquet facilities in Springfield. Miss Miller is a part of the Inn at 835, and she will no doubt continue to add to the luxurious mystique and charm of the old inn.

# THE SPLIT-HOUSE HAUNTING

It was 1935, and the Great Depression was not yet over in Springfield. Gertrude and Raymond Meyers were newlyweds in their twenties when they moved into their modest home late that summer. Their house looked similar to all the other houses in the neighborhood, but it looked exactly like the house right next door. The newlyweds were just grateful to have a roof over their heads in such hard times.

Gertrude was a high school teacher with an ambition to be a writer someday. Raymond was a night laborer as a printer, and he was gone most evenings. They didn't have much time together, as one was coming home from work while the other was leaving for work. Gertrude had to spend her evenings home alone until three thirty in the morning, when Raymond came home, and this made for some lonely nights.

With fall settling in and the air growing cooler, it was time to close up the windows in the house in preparation for the coming winter. Raymond was still working late, but they were lucky to both have jobs, so the newlyweds did what they had to do to make ends meet. Gertrude was feeling down since she wasn't able to have the windows open, allowing in a breeze and the outside noises to keep her company on those lonely evenings. Now, with the house closed up, Gertrude became more aware of her surroundings. Something was different about the house, and it made her uncomfortable. Gertrude sensed there was a presence in the house. She was not as alone as she had previously thought, and this unwelcome presence was not good company

Night after night, Gertrude closed her bedroom door and climbed into a cold and empty bed. And then the phantom walker would begin his nightly torment. At ten thirty almost every night, she heard heavy footsteps start at the front door, walk across the front hall and methodically climb the stairs. They would walk right to her bedroom door and suddenly stop. She would wake from her sleep, hide under the covers and painstakingly listen to the phantom footsteps; by the time they reached her bedroom door, she was paralyzed with fear. She sensed it was a man because the footsteps were so heavy. The phantom walker didn't show every night, much to her relief, but when he did, it was always at ten thirty sharp. Nevertheless, Gertrude began to wake every night at ten thirty in anticipation of the phantom walker, and she began to lose sleep.

Gertrude was reluctant to tell her husband anything, as she didn't want him to think she was ridiculous or making it up because she was lonely at night. But the stalker was unnerving her, and it was getting to be too much to bear. She had to do something. Gertrude decided to summon her strength and courage and confront the phantom walker the next time he reached her bedroom door. Just as expected, at ten thirty sharp the footsteps began. She heard every step coming closer to her door, and then the footsteps stopped right at the threshold of her door. With all her might, she yanked the door open and found no one there. She looked down the hall, but it was empty. For the next week, every time Gertrude heard the phantom footsteps stop at her door, she opened the door, hoping to see who the phantom walker was. No one was ever there.

While Gertrude was dealing with this, Raymond had been having his own inexplicable experiences with the phantom footsteps. He usually got home from work at about three thirty in the morning and would first go down into the basement to stoke up the coal furnace before going to bed. While down in the basement, he would hear footsteps walking across the floor above him, and he wondered what his wife was doing up so late. But he would find her moments later fast asleep in their bed. Raymond, sleeping late, also heard the footsteps in the morning outside their bedroom door after his wife had left for work.

Raymond decided to ask his wife if she ever got up in the night and came downstairs while he was stoking the furnace in the basement. He told her about the footsteps, and she was relieved to finally be able to tell him about the phantom walker that tortured her almost nightly. Their stories were similar—always hearing the footsteps but never seeing anyone. They were both curious who the phantom walker was and why he was here.

Winter came and went, and the phantom walker persisted. Gertrude and Raymond gradually became used to the footsteps and weren't so unnerved by their phantom walker anymore, but they still wondered who he was. A possible answer would soon come to them.

Spring arrived, and Gertrude was happy to have the windows open again, with the sun shining in and warming the house. She decided to plant a garden to occupy her time after school. One day while working in her garden, Gertrude was talking with her next-door neighbors, who were also working in their garden. A grandmother and grandson lived in the identical house next door. They got to talking about their houses and how they were identical. Gertrude mentioned the phantom walker that had belabored them since they moved in late the previous summer. The neighbors were amazed to hear of the footsteps because they, too, had been experiencing the same haunting in their own house for some time now. The phantom walker followed the same routine in both houses. The footsteps began at the front door at ten thirty and walked across the hall and then up the stairs to the master bedroom door. And just like in the Meyers' house, the neighbors only heard the footsteps every couple of nights and never saw anyone.

The neighbor told Gertrude that their houses had been joined together at one time, making it a duplex. The owner of the duplex house had committed suicide at some point. The new property owner decided, for whatever reason, to split the duplex apart, making it two separate houses.

They all decided that the mysterious phantom night walker was probably the former owner who had committed suicide. Now, with his former house split into two separate homes, perhaps he couldn't decide which house to haunt, so in death he alternated, haunting each half of his old house on different nights.

The haunting continued on for years and gradually dissipated over time. The phantom walker is heard no more.

# THE GHOSTLY EDWARDS PLACE

E dwards Place was built in 1833 for Dr. Thomas Houghan, but he sold the story-and-a-half home and fifteen acres of land to Benjamin and Helen Edwards in 1843. The Edwardses renovated the home, adding fifteen rooms to create its present-day appearance. The beautiful Italianate-style mansion is well preserved. It is the oldest house in Springfield on its original foundation and arguably the oldest house in the city today.

Benjamin Edwards was part of a prominent social and political family in Springfield. His father, Ninian Edwards, was the first territorial governor of Illinois and later a senator and governor. The lawyer's family had status, wealth and plenty of political power. Benjamin's older brother, Albert, was the founder of A.G. Edwards, and his other older brother, Ninian W. Edwards, was a state politician who married Elizabeth Todd, Mary Todd's sister.

When Mary Todd came to Springfield, she moved in with her sister Elizabeth and brother-in-law. That Edwards home was once located at Second and Jackson Streets but was razed in 1918 to make way for the Howlett Building. Mary, who was brought up in high society back in Lexington, was immediately brought into the elite social circle of Springfield and certainly attended dinner parties at Edwards Place. Later, Mary was introduced to a man named Abraham Lincoln, most likely at the home of Ninian and Elizabeth, where they courted each other before their marriage. The famous "courting couch," once in the parlor of the Edwards home, is now kept at Edwards Place and is on display today. Mary Lincoln and Helen Edwards were good friends and shared that bond for life.

Edwards Place was one of several Springfield homes that were host to Springfield's social elite events and parties. Along with lavish dinner parties, Edwards Place was host to scores of picnics on the grounds during the summers. Matters of high society were a part of entertaining in those days. The men might be in a parlor smoking cigars and discussing the latest politics while the women were in another room engaged in the latest courtship gossip. However, it would be no surprise to find Mary Lincoln in the parlor with the men debating politics. She was a woman ahead of her time. Abraham Lincoln and Ben Edwards were more than relatives; they ran in the same social and political circles. The Lincolns and Edwardses both held fantastic dinner parties, and they were guests in one another's homes on numerous occasions. Both men were attorneys, and they had faced each other in court over four hundred times, though sometimes they worked together as co-counsel. Though both men were Whigs, they did not agree on matters of politics. When the Whig Party dissolved in the mid-1850s, Lincoln became a Republican and Edwards became a Democrat. Ben Edwards supported Stephen Douglas and held political rallies for him at Edwards Place during the 1858 senatorial campaign.

To learn about what it would have been like to socialize with Abraham and Mary Lincoln, you need only to walk through the front door of Edwards Place, now owned by the Springfield Art Association. The historical interpretation of Edwards Place today tells the story of Benjamin and Helen Edwards, their connection to the Lincoln family and their lavish social lifestyle from 1843 to 1909. The home is an open-air museum where you can walk through the entire house amongst an amazing collection of nineteenth-century antique furnishings. The old mansion has a sensational history, and within the walls of Edwards Place are old ghosts.

Edwards Place hosts an annual Halloween event called Haunted Nights of History where site interpreters dress up as Edwards family members and, while stationed throughout the house, tell stories about the home and the family to visitors. But the ghosts in Edwards Place find ways to make their presence known and, in some cases, tell their own stories.

The strange and ghostly encounters at Edwards Place are believed to be the result of several different entities haunting the old mansion. There is thought to be the spirit of an indentured servant who once lived and worked in the home. Also, the grandchildren of Benjamin and Helen Edwards, Tom and Alice, may be haunting the house, reliving their youth.

During one of the Haunted Nights of History events, there were several visitors who suddenly felt ill when they reached the top of the stairs, and

The first-floor parlor of the ghostly Edwards Place, now haunted by the grandchildren of the Benjamin Edwards family.

they had to immediately retreat outside for fresh air. People claimed that they felt an unseen presence at the top of the second floor stairs and in the bedroom to the right off the stairs. Voice recordings made in this area revealed a young girl's voice that said her name was "Alice," and she was apparently not too fond of her bed coverings. People not only sensed her little girl spirit in the room, but also some claimed to have felt a tug on their shirt or coat. On at least one occasion, a visitor to the home reported seeing the ghostly apparition of a woman in that very room looking out the window. The witness first thought she was a costumed interpreter dressed in period clothing, but when the woman in the old dress disappeared after a brief moment, she realized that she had just seen someone from days long past.

But the playful spirit of Tom is one of the most interactive spirits I've ever encountered. Tom likes to hang out in the back parlor of the home, which is filled with antique children's toys. What ghost boy wouldn't want to hang out in the most fun room in the house? If there was ever any doubt as to the existence of young Tom, it was laid to rest when a voice recording was made in the playroom, capturing the young boy's ghostly voice answering direct questions. One evening, there were eight people sitting in a circle on the playroom floor. Someone asked if Tom was present. No response was audibly heard, but when the recording was later played back, the chilling response was clear: "Tom has come to play."

Ben and Helen had grandchildren named Tom and Alice. Though neither child died in the home, their presence in the home has been recorded. Both grandchildren lived through adulthood, so why might they be haunting Edwards Place as children? Is this even possible? For many kids, childhood was a magical time, especially for kids who were surrounded by loving parents and family. Childhood was an innocent time not yet tainted by the troubles of the world. And Edwards Place was a lively home with lots of excitement and events going on, especially those summer picnics. But if there are kid ghosts around Edwards Place, they would certainly need supervision.

Staff members have been repeatedly called at night to Edwards Place to reset the tripped motion sensor alarm. The alarm is usually tripped in

The playroom, where the grandchildren still play, is full of nineteenth-century children's toys. This is the room where a voice recording once picked up a little boy's voice saying, "Tom has come to play."

the kitchen, breakfast and dining area, where a servant would have spent considerable time. As many times as the alarm has been tripped, no one has ever been found in the home, and there is no sign of attempted entry. The motion sensors are always found to be in good working order.

Visitors to the home have time and again randomly made comments of feeling a presence, as though someone unseen were standing in the dining area where inexplicable cold spots were experienced. During one cold spot experience, witnesses claimed to have seen a white wisp of light streak across a doorway. Voice recordings made in the area reveal a young woman's soft, unintelligible voice; to some, it sounds like she might be African American. But if this is the spirit of a servant in the home, she is also encountered in the attic. The sense of an unseen presence really kicks in for some people when going up the stairs to the attic where the servants' quarters were once located. The remains of the old servant call system can still be seen today. Also seen in the attic is a bizarre bottle cap–sized white light, called a sprite, zipping through the air in random patterns that abruptly change directions. The mystery light is seen for several seconds before zipping away and disappearing from sight.

The Edwardses did host an indentured servant for one year in the house. Perhaps after that year, indentured servitude did not sit well with the Edwardses, and they began to employ Irish housekeeping staff. The indentured help was African American, and she did not receive pay, but she was given room and board. It's hard to say why she might be haunting Edwards Place. A life of servitude is a hard and unglamorous life, but could it be she formed a bond with the children and remains in the house looking after them?

Perhaps as time passes, more haunting evidence will present itself to explain the nature of the Edwards Place hauntings.

# THE VIRGIL HICKOX HOUSE
# AND NORB ANDY'S

Virgil Hickox was born in 1806 in Jefferson County, New York, three years before Abraham Lincoln. He came to Springfield in 1834, and by 1839, he had married his wife, Marie Catharine Cabanis, and built a home on Capitol Avenue between Fifth and Sixth Streets. Hickox fathered ten children, but only six survived. Today, the old Hickox House may be the oldest residential structure still standing in downtown Springfield. Though the home has had several renovations, it retains much of its original architectural features inside and out. The home holds an amazing amount of Springfield history and may be regarded as one of the most haunted homes in the city today. Scores of people have experienced the haunted history of the Hickox House over time. Some of the haunted activity is downright frightful and even violent on occasion.

Hickox had only an elementary school–level education, but he became an entrepreneur of all sorts, investing in his own mercantile store and becoming president of Springfield's Saving Bank and founder of the Chicago-Alton Railroad. He also cofounded the town of Lincoln, Illinois. Hickox was an important political figure, acting as chairman of the Democratic State Committee. But the only political office he held was canal commissioner of the Chicago and Michigan Canal, the largest nineteenth-century canal in the United States. Hickox was a Democrat and good friends with Stephen Douglas, who visited the Hickox home on occasion. It's likely that Lincoln was received here as well. Hickox worked as Douglas's campaign manager in the 1858 senatorial bid against Abraham Lincoln and said his greatest

*Above*: The old Virgil Hickox House as it appeared just after the turn of the century.

*Left*: This photo, taken on Memorial Day in 1887, shows Civil War soldiers standing along the street in front of the old Hickox House.

life accomplishment was Douglas's success. Nevertheless, Hickox and Lincoln were cordial to each other like gentlemen. Virgil Hickox held the last letter dictated by Stephen Douglas, dated May 10, 1861, in which Douglas declared that there could be only two political parties, one of patriots and the other of traitors. Douglas also advised his friends to lay down any views that would impede the preservation of the Union.

Virgil Hickox.

After the death of Virgil Hickox in February 1880, his stately Capitol Avenue home began its long connection to Springfield's cultural fabric. In 1890, the home became the first site for the Sangamo Club, a sort of country club–type organization. After World War I, the Sangamo Club moved to a new location, and the home's new tenant was the Sangamon County coroner, who lived upstairs and ran his own funeral home downstairs and in the basement, where the embalming procedures took place. The basement window where coffins, and perhaps even bodies, were slid inside remains today. During the days of Prohibition, the basement was used as a speakeasy. After Prohibition was over, the old speakeasy became a legal establishment. A popular Cheers-style restaurant and tavern called Norb Andy's Tabarin opened its doors, and for the next nearly fifty years, Norb's was a favorite watering hole of the politicians down the street. Imagine the tales this house could tell— the heated politics of Lincoln's day, the fellowship of a country club, the preservation and mourning of the dead, the drunken debauchery of the old speakeasy and the good times and bonds made between friends at Norb Andy's Tabarin.

The haunted activity in this old house is incredible, and you might think it results from the old mortuary once here, but the home seems to be haunted by a variety of spirits, many of which are not necessarily connected to the house. This suggests that the home may contain a portal of sorts, an open window between two planes of existence that allows spirits to stream back and forth.

The Hickox House has been widely investigated for several years by a number of paranormal groups, yielding a good amount of haunting evidence. Most convincing are the voice recordings made in the house. Strange noises—like whispering, tapping, knocking, doors closing and even footsteps—appear on digital recorders, but when actual voices appear on the recorder in response to direct questions, it's pretty convincing that the paranormal is present. Recorded responses such as "I'm dead," "Go away," "Talking," "Mother," "Where is it," "Yes" and "No" can be heard. There was one very unsettling recording that sends chills up the spine when played back. A guttural voice said, "Not dead."

Orbs of light show up in lots of photos taken in the house, but of course most orbs can be explained away as dust particles, pollen, other particles in the air or especially camera lens or flash artifact. But in the Hickox House, orbs of light can be seen with the naked eye, and often times the orb is seen traveling through the air for a brief second or two before disappearing from sight. On rare occasions, a strange, smoky, foglike mist that appears to be dimensional has been caught on camera, and on at least two occasions, it has made its presence visible to people touring through the house.

There seem to be a number of child spirits in the house from time to time, but few of them seem to have any connection to the house. Sensitive people suggest they were brought here in death because of the other children already here. But aside from an open portal, why would they be here? When the funeral home opened for business in the old Hickox House, Springfield was still recovering from the infamous flu epidemic of 1918, which affected thousands and killed about 350 citizens. Springfield was under quarantine, and temporary hospitals were set up around town to take on the overflow of patients. The death rate was still above normal for several months afterward, and funeral homes were still busy. Though the epidemic hit all ages, it was children who were hardest hit by the killer flu of 1918. Some suggest the children are lost, and they may be right in at least one case. There are several voice recordings made on different dates that suggest little twelve-year-old Alice is looking for her mother. Efforts made to cross her over into the light have not been successful, and she remains in the house. When asked about other spirits in the house, the child's voice on the recording simply states, "Afraid."

It's believed that Alice is referring to the shadow man that seems to be a dominant spirit in the house. The spirit children are frightened of him, and at times so are the living. The shadow man is arrogant and does not like intruders in his space. He's been known to choke tour guides for bringing groups through the house, and he's attacked the patrons as well. One night, a Springfield firefighter was slapped in the face by an unseen hand. No one around him saw anyone slap him, but the red handprint was clear on his face. Astonished, he said, "I felt the sting. It hurt!" But this firefighter isn't the first one to have been slapped by the shadow man; it's happened to several others as well. Little is known about the shadow man, whose dark presence still roams the house, but it is believed he was a temperamental person in life.

As for the Hickox family haunting their old house, there has been some contact made with Marie, Virgil's wife, and one of the children named Mary. But spirits seem to come and go from the Hickox House, making every investigation unique, and the Hickox family seems to remain in the background.

The portal in the home remains open, but now it's believed that St. Peter stands vigilant guard over the portal window, helping lost spirits find their way home into the light.

Norb Andy's Tabarin was opened in 1937 by a salty man named Norbert Anderson. He was never in the navy, but Norb, as everyone called him, had blue eyes and a weathered smile. He always liked the fisherman décor of taverns back East, and he fancied the same décor in his tabarin. The nautical décor of knotted pine, fishnets, buoys and whale oil lamps, along with Norb's warm hospitality, gave Norb Andy's something few establishments have: tradition.

It was Norb's personality that gave this place life. Patrons here knew each other well, and Norb knew most of his patrons by name. He warmly greeted his customers and thanked them when they left, and in no time, he had a strong and faithful clientele. The loyal bar staff and equally loyal customers were the best of friends, and it was the best of times—drunken nights of good drinks, good music, good food and good friends. It really was a Cheers type of place. Customers could come in, get a great meal or a stiff drink for a good price and sit in a chair that may have been occupied by well-known politicians, such as former governors James Thompson, Adlai Stevenson and Henry Horner or Secretary of State Alan Dixon, just to name a few. In fact, Norb's had a small back room where politicians would hold unofficial and casual meetings with other politicians. It was appropriately called the scuttlebutt room. Along with politicians and lobbyists, Springfield attorneys would meet at Norb's for happy hour. And if you asked Norb what his customers drank, he would tell you they don't drink; they come for the food. Norb was protective of his high-end customers.

Norb's had become a Springfield institution. It was *the* place to go. Old Norb loved his place, and he ran it for forty-plus years. When old Norb finally died, it was the end of an era for this neighborhood bar. Last call had passed, and the party was over.

When this place was reopened as Norb Andy's some years ago, the party was back on. People were delighted to have the old neighborhood bar open, and they returned for another stretch of good drinks, good music, good food and, of course, good friends. The new Norb's kept its old décor and charm. It's believed that old Norb himself returned to the party as well, pulling pranks on the customers, perhaps to let folks know he's still around, looking after his old tabarin.

Numerous heart-jumping, strange and inexplicable things have gone on here. Granted, there is alcohol involved, but there are as many stories told by the sober. Apparently, Norb is quite the prankster.

Patrons engaged in conversation reach for their drinks to find their glass moved or even switched with another patron's drink. Glasses get moved around on the bar as well. Bartenders tell stories of setting a new drink down on the waitress station mat, and when the waitress goes to retrieve the drink, she finds the drink gone—not empty but missing. While you might be tempted to say this is a customer or waitress playing a prank on the bartender, most bartenders are savvy enough to not repeatedly fall for this. Norb is believed to switch bottles of booze around so when the bartender reaches for a particular bottle, she finds a different bottle in its place.

One of the more frightful pranks by Norb involves people utilizing the restrooms. Patrons joke with other patrons to not look in the mirror while in the restroom or you might meet old Norb himself. Patrons using the restrooms sometimes dismiss the challenge to not look in the mirror and have at times regretted their decision. Once in a while, when looking into the mirror, customers are startled to see a man standing behind them, but when they quickly turn around, no one is there. This is especially heart thumping for the ladies meeting Norb in the women's restroom. People have been known to literally run out of the restroom, anxious and disheveled, much to the amusement of other patrons. Norb has been seen in the bar area by both patrons and employees. But Norb's ghostly apparition is quite unique.

It's believed that Norb frequently wore some sort of blue polyester leisure suit or sports coat when working at his establishment. People say the man looks real enough, but his suit, at certain angles, seems to give off a bluish glow. After hours, while cleaning up, the bar employees have seen Norb's ghostly bluish apparition walking up the stairs leaving for the night. Some

The Hickox House and Norb Andy's as the home appears today.

employees are amused enough to call out, "Goodnight, Norb!" Even patrons have seen Norb pass by the doorway of the scuttlebutt room. He's also been spotted sitting on the corner barstool at the bar, which was apparently the stool he frequently occupied.

One new young bartender opening the bar up for the afternoon crowd had a frightful encounter with Norb. She had been open for just a few minutes and didn't hear anyone come in, but she turned around and was startled by a man sitting on the corner barstool. He was wearing an unfashionable blue sports coat. She was on her way to retrieve a new bottle from storage, and she told the man she'd be right back. He didn't say a word. When she came back a moment later, the man was gone. She thought that was weird. She was jolted a moment later, though. As she looked at the spot where the man was sitting, her eyes fell upon the picture on the wall. It was the same man, and she knew the man in the picture was old Norb Andy himself in the very same blue sports coat. He had been dead for some time. She commented that she could even still smell his aftershave. The shaken girl waited outside until other patrons came in before going back inside.

I've had my own encounter with Norb as well. It was about 3:30 p.m. and the bar had just opened. There were a couple people sitting at the far side of the bar; the bartender was behind the bar, and I was standing at the corner of the bar. I had walked past the picture of Norb on the wall numerous times before. Chatting with the bartender, I started asking about Norb and the picture. The two patrons at the bar start telling stories of Norb's ghostly pranks. Literally seconds into the conversation, a stack of menus on the corner right next to me suddenly flew across the room and smacked against the wall with pretty good force. I nearly fell over. All our mouths were agape! Now, these menus weren't precariously stacked, and they didn't just fall over fanning out across the floor. These menus flew across the room a good ten feet and hit the wall. After a moment of silence and bewilderment, we all began to laugh.

At the end of Norb's life, he just couldn't give up his bar and all the good friends he had made in the place. For me, there is no doubt that Norbert Anderson still haunts his old tavern out of a bond with his establishment and the Shangri-La it represents for him. For Norb, the good times continue, and it seems he's got plenty of ghostly friends in the Hickox House these days.

# THE OLD HUTCHINSON CEMETERY AND SPRINGFIELD HIGH SCHOOL

The legend begins with a custodian checking for a water leak in the basement of the school. Suddenly, in the dim light, he saw a young girl of about ten years old in a flowered dress standing amongst a group of pipes, looking at him. Thinking one of the students was goofing off, but noticing her strange appearance, he rebuked her presence. "What are you doing down here? You're not supposed to be down here." And without a sound, she vanished into thin air right before his eyes.

Springfield High School is built directly on the site of the old Hutchinson Cemetery of the 1800s. John Hutchinson was a cabinetmaker and undertaker. In 1843, he started a small family cemetery on a plot of land he owned. There was a small city cemetery just a block over; however, the Hutchinson Cemetery soon became the formal burial ground for the town of Springfield, eventually covering six acres of land and containing around seven hundred known graves. The most notable person buried in the cemetery was no doubt Eddie Lincoln, son of Abraham Lincoln, who died of an illness approaching his fourth birthday in 1850. Amongst the graves of Springfield's early pioneers are quite a number of child burials. Even the historical marker in front of the high school mentions the high number of child burials within the old cemetery.

The Capitol City was still a rough prairie town at the time, and life without many conveniences was hard, even harsh. Accidents were common. Records list that one child was scalded to death, and another was killed when struck by lightning. Disease was difficult to control, and Springfield was hit hard

The historical plaque out in front of Springfield High School talks about the high number of child burials in the old cemetery. The history also mentions that likely not all graves were removed, and today the high school sits directly on the site of the Hutchinson Cemetery.

several times by measles epidemics. The bringer of death had no prejudices, as children were often hit the hardest by disease. A fever raging through a community would instill fear, and everyone was in danger, as there was little knowledge of how to stop the epidemic. It was not uncommon for cemeteries to receive multiple or mass burials in a single day when a fever belabored a community. The dead would be wrapped up in the sheets they died in and buried at night so the public would not attend the funerals. Clothes and possessions, and sometimes their homes, would be burned to stop the spread of the disease. Great numbers of pioneer and early families had gaps in their families from losing one or more family members, just like the Lincoln family.

However, in 1876, a new city ordinance prevented any further burials within the new city limits. Rather than just close the cemetery and simply not allow any more burials, it was decided to remove the entire cemetery from within city limits. Thus began the removal of six hundred corpses to their new places of burial. Bodies were reinterred in different cemeteries, but the majority of the corpses were reinterred in Oak Ridge Cemetery north of town. However, some of the older folks of Springfield who had gathered and watched the disinterment claim that the number of corpses removed did not match the number of burials recorded in the cemetery, believing that some of the dead remain. It is quite possible that some of the graves of the poor, unknown and indigent were not moved. The historical plaque in front of the school acknowledges that not all graves were moved. It's possible that not all of the grave locations were known due to lost grave records or even poor record keeping. Also, bodies buried in pine boxes would have decayed rapidly, leaving little trace of the burial. A more sinister reason for the lack of complete removal was that whoever was paying the bill for the disinterment was trying to save money by leaving a hundred or so graves behind.

With the corpses moved to Oak Ridge Cemetery, the Hutchinson land remained empty. Investors and developers, as you might expect, were reluctant to build on the land knowing its history. The city finally stepped in and developed the land to be Forest Park. And though it was now a beautiful city park, people were reluctant to use the park knowing its macabre history. Eventually, people began to use the park, having Sunday afternoon picnics on the old cemetery grounds. Finally, in 1917, the school board acquired the land and subsequently built the Beaux Arts–style high school that still stands today. The school building retains much of its impressive original mosaics and architectural features.

But what if there were graves left behind? Though no stories of ever finding skeletal remains have been reported on the property, it is not unthinkable that remains could have been found when the school was built, and any remains discovered would have been quietly moved or even disposed of. Perhaps remains still exist on the grounds and simply have yet to be found.

One might think the school would have been haunted ever since its construction, but it wasn't until the elevator shaft was dug in 1983 that things start to get a little strange in the halls of Springfield High. Workers were using a small backhoe to dig out the shaft, and in the bucket of the last scoop of dirt that came up was what they thought was a large rock. After clearing away the dirt, they found a small tombstone. With the stone worn by time, the only legible words read, "Our Daughter" on the top and "Cut down but not destroyed" carved into the side, suggesting a girl who died young, perhaps from an illness or accident.

With the tombstone uncovered, the hauntings began.

The ghostly little girl has appeared to numerous witnesses over the years in various parts of the school, oftentimes in the basement mechanical rooms and in the utility tunnels under the school. But all kinds of ghostly activity have been reported by witnesses all over the high school. Skeptics often claim that the haunted stories are the result of a student's active imagination or someone seeking attention, and the stories have just perpetuated over the years. One might expect students to come up with their own imaginative stories of sinister encounters, but there are plenty of teachers, custodians and maintenance workers who speak of ghostly and bizarre encounters. These people tend to be in the building later in the evening and sometimes work alone or with few people around, providing a more conducive environment for a paranormal encounter than a full classroom or a bustling hallway full of kids, for example. Nevertheless, as a result of the nerve-wracking but harmless encounters with the ghostly little girl, she has been affectionately named Rachel by the students at the school, though her actual name may never be known.

One day, there were a couple of plumbers who were apparently working on a water leak in the basement of the high school during school hours. One of the plumbers was inside a utility tunnel hunched over working on pipes when he turned around and encountered a little girl in a flowered dress with eyelets. Startled by her sudden appearance and confused as to why one of the students was down in the basement, he nervously scolded her and told her she needed to go back upstairs. The girl appeared to be about ten years old. She turned around and walked out of the tunnel. The worker followed her out of the tunnel and watched her walk around the corner, where his partner was working. Concerned, he turned the corner and asked his partner, "Where'd the girl go?" His partner's reply was, "What girl?"

An electrician doing some work saw the ghostly apparition of the little girl while working in the basement utility tunnels. He made haste in leaving the building, in front of students and staff out in the halls during class change. Some say his face was as white as a ghost! Witnesses say he briskly walked straight for the nearest exit with determination, knocking people out of his way. Apparently, the electrician did not come back to complete the work.

Rachel's ghostly specter has been seen wandering the halls in the evening when there are few people around. One teacher working late in the evening on a club project was walking back to the classroom from the restroom when she saw a ghostly figure glide past at the end of the hall. Every footstep would have echoed in the empty hallway, but there was no sound. She had heard the stories of Rachel and gave it little thought over the years, but now, bewildered by her own encounter, Rachel was real. Other students and teachers also speak of hearing phantom footsteps echoing in the empty halls. The footsteps seem to suddenly stop when someone calls out, "Who's there?"

The strangeness doesn't stop here. Teachers and students in or near the home economics room complain of sudden cold spots and inexplicable brushes of air. Most unnerving is an ominous sound—like someone exhaling a loud single, throaty, heavy breath of air. The sound is known as the "death rattle" in the medical community, a deep throaty rattle as a dying person exhales his final breath of air. One teacher jokingly said it sounded like Darth Vader with a cold exhaling, but he always attributed the sound to wind blowing down the empty hallway. Teachers and students alike speak of strange whispers of wind in the haunted halls of the high school.

Certainly, old buildings do make strange but explainable noises. Buildings settle; old boilers and pipes knock, clink and even rattle. Wind coming in the smallest hole can make a variety of ominous sounds. But perhaps not all sounds can be attributed to the old building and its mechanics.

The book room seems to be the center for more ghostly activity. Teachers work in the room sorting and requisitioning textbooks for classes. Shadowy figures, cold spots and brief and gentle wisps of wind occur there, but there are also phantom sounds of the doors opening and closing that unnerve some teachers enough that they quickly leave the room. One teacher spoke of hearing the death rattle and seeing a dark shadowy figure standing among the bookshelves. She felt a panic to get out of the room. "Whatever it was, it didn't want me in there. I don't go there alone anymore." And though some find the ghostly encounters unnerving and frightful, others find them playful.

A former teacher mentioned a time when he had set a stack of books down on a table, turned to pick up another stack of books, turned back around to place the new stack next to the first stack and, to his amazement, found the single stack split into two stacks. Other teachers speak of similar experiences.

But what about the elevator where Rachel's tombstone was found? It seems to malfunction at times, but it always passes inspection. Frequently, when someone approaches the elevator to press the call button, the doors suddenly open before the call button is pressed. The doors open and no one is there, or patrons are taken to different floors than the floor summoned. Elevator inspectors are at a loss to explain why this occurs. Custodians in the building have become so used to the elevator doors opening upon approach that they simply reply, "Thanks, Rachel."

People riding the elevator sometimes report being unusually unnerved and uncomfortable, sensing they're not alone. There was an electrician who had been to the school a number of times and had encountered Rachel one time too many. Hence, he always refused to ride the elevator. He would put his toolbox on the elevator and send his tools up while he took the stairs.

For as many times as the elevator doors open and no one is seen coming out, there are a number of occasions in which Rachel's ghostly apparition *is* seen walking off the elevator and turning the corner. Those brave enough to follow her around the corner are astonished to find an empty hallway.

But is it Rachel? No doubt, Rachel's grave was not the only one left behind. It would stand to reason that not all the ghostly activity in the halls of Springfield High School results from her restless spirit.

In the vicinity of the Hutchinson Cemetery, there were several other cemeteries, such as the previously mentioned city cemetery a block to the east. But there was also a Catholic cemetery nearby and several other smaller cemeteries comprising a single grave to small family plots. However, because of the new city ordinance, all graves had to be moved outside city limits. And since it's known that not all graves were removed from the Hutchinson Cemetery, it would be reasonable to believe that not all graves were removed from some of the other cemeteries.

There is at least one account that comes from the old city cemetery site. The site is now occupied by modern buildings and a parking area. An employee of one of the businesses there had left work and was getting into his small SUV, as he had done five days a week for a couple of years. But on this occasion, he put his vehicle in reverse, about to back out, checked his rear-view mirror and was suddenly startled by a dark figure that appeared to be right behind his vehicle. He quickly turned his head to see who was behind him and saw nothing.

Perhaps there may be other Rachels out there, wandering the streets of Springfield or haunting buildings, searching endlessly for their lost graves from nearly a century and a half ago.

# THE GHOST OF RUDY

Prohibition was over in 1933, and since then, Americans have been turned on to legal nightclubbing. No longer did patrons go in the through the back door to sneak a drink in a speakeasy. The 1940s ushered in a new era of nightclubbing made popular and trendy by the lifestyles of Hollywood movie stars and famous musicians. The hottest nightclub between Chicago and St. Louis was a place called the Lake Club in Springfield, once located on Fox Bridge Road. Owners Hugo Giovagnoli and Harold Henderson, both of whom had star quality themselves, operated the club from 1940 through 1968. The Lake Club served fine food and stiff drinks, but it had top billing entertainment to attract customers as well. People also came to the club for the thrill of illegal gambling. Behind a steel door was a secret gambling den, where patrons could play all kinds of games. The owners used the gambling profits to pay the high cost of the top-billing performers of the day.

A litany of stars came to Springfield just for the party and to perform at the Lake Club: Ella Fitzgerald, Mel Tormé, Frank Sinatra Jr., Paul Lynde, Joey Bishop, Nat "King" Cole, Dick and Jerry Van Dyke, Guy Lombardo, Lawrence Welk, Pearl Bailey, Bob Hope, Chico Marx and the list goes on. Friends of famous performers were also known to stop in for the party. Mickey Rooney once showed up just for dinner and drinks and unintentionally stole the show. Needless to say, the crowd was always to capacity at the Lake Club. It was the place to be, and times were good.

However, behind the glitz and glamour, there were problems for the owners of the club. They sometimes took chances on the entertainment.

The Lake Club as it appeared in its heyday.

Once they paid a group called the Vagabonds $15,000 to play at the club for a week, but they only recouped $2,000. But the problems went beyond bad entertainment decisions.

Though gambling was illegal, it was somewhat tolerated at the time. After the failure of Prohibition, the law was not overly motivated to crack down on illegal backroom gambling dens. Besides, the Lake Club was far from the only place with a secret gambling operation in Springfield at the time. Dozens of illegal backroom gambling dens could be found in any number of taverns throughout the old Levee District along Washington Street. However, in the 1950s, a new era of social responsibility encouraged law enforcement to crack down on illegal activities. One night, an undercover state trooper lost $128 playing dice in the illegal backroom gambling den at the club. Several days later, at two o'clock in the morning, state police raided the back room and seized all the gambling items, such as a pool table turned over and used as a gambling table, playing cards, dice, IOUs and gambling records. The gambling room was so well hidden that patrons in the club area were never aware that a raid had taken place! The state police raid would be the death knell for the club.

Without the gambling profits, the owners couldn't pay for the high-priced entertainment, so they were forced to hire third-billing performers, who

The dining room and main stage, where great numbers of famous entertainers performed to a packed house for thirty years.

didn't attract as many customers. Also, with the gambling gone, the thrill was gone too.

Lawsuits plagued the owners and contributed to the eventual decline of the Lake Club. One lady cut her hand on a broken ashtray and sued for $23,000. A dancer slipped on stage and sued for $60,000. Irving Berlin and some other musicians sued the club for using their music without proper copyright licensing. A comedian named Willie Shore was killed in a car accident after leaving the club one night, and his wife sued the club. A patron sued after falling down in an over-capacity crowd. On top of all the lawsuits, the owners had to pay thousands of dollars in back taxes.

The 1960s brought in a new era of entertainment. The classy, sophisticated nightclub scene with more intimate entertainment was giving way to venues offering crowds of people loud rock 'n' roll bands. Henderson and Giovagnoli just couldn't keep up with the fast-paced and competitive nightclub business. So after twenty-eight years, they turned off the stage lights and microphones for the final time in 1968. Henderson and Giovagnoli still maintained ownership of the building until their deaths in 1977 and 1988, respectively.

Through the 1970s, there were attempts to revive the Lake Club. New club owners Tom and Bill opened the Sober Duck Disco and Rock Club and promoted good drinks and quality entertainment like the old Lake Club. Not long after opening the new venue, the drinks were flowing and the bands were jamming on stage, but almost right away strange things began to happen.

Tom said that the strange things were minor at first, and he didn't pay much attention to them. But then he'd start hearing and seeing things, and he would try to rationalize that it was nothing or that it was just the pipes or the building making strange noises. But the thing he just couldn't dismiss was an eerie, cold chill that would take over a room or breeze by. He said it was a chill that ran right down deep and that he could literally feel his hair standing straight up. He said it was the "worst thing," and he *knew* there was something going on in the club.

Bill recalled his bizarre encounter with a phantom piano player that convinced him of a ghost haunting the club. He had come into the club about noon one day and sat down at the bar. The lights were off, so it was still a bit dark in there. Out of nowhere, the piano in the back storeroom started playing. Bill thought one of the musicians had come in early to practice, but it sounded terrible, so he thought he would go back there and see who was playing. He walked down the hall to the back storeroom, and as soon as he arrived at the doorway of the room and looked inside, the music stopped. He didn't see anyone around, just the piano. A cold chill ran right up Bill's spine.

Tom and Bill used a back room as their private office space. Almost right away, they both felt uneasy when in the office. That eerie chill would take over the office at times, and they would have a weird feeling that someone else was there watching them. Bill had a large trained dog that would sometimes cower down as if sensing something in the room. Electronic equipment in the office would occasionally go haywire; for example, the adding machine would sometimes suddenly turn on by itself or go crazy printing out numbers.

Owners and employees would hear phantom footsteps in the hallway leading from the bar area to the back office, but no one was ever seen in the hall. The footsteps would come right up to the threshold of the office door and suddenly stop. One employee in the hall going to the back office once saw a dark shadow in the light up ahead and heard footsteps walking right in front of her toward the office. Thinking it was one of the owners she was looking for, she called out his name but got no response. Suddenly, she didn't feel well and just wanted to get out of there.

There was once a bartender who went into the kitchen to get a cup of coffee. There's a big heavy steel kitchen door that takes a little effort to open and close. He got his coffee and left the empty kitchen, but as he passed through the doorway, the heavy steel door closed right behind him. He didn't go back for a second cup.

Everyone working at the club suspected they had a ghost haunting the Sober Duck, and it didn't take much research to conclude who their resident ghost might be.

A bartender named Albert "Rudy" Cranor, who had been living in a small second-floor apartment, stayed on at the club to do routine maintenance and look after the building after it closed in 1968. He was a large man with a full head of gray hair. Customers knew him as Rudy, and he had worked at the club for quite a long time. He was a popular bartender with the customers and the stars, and he sometimes took them into a small private backroom bar for cigars and drinks. August Busch was one of Rudy's favorite and best customers. Rudy had seen it all, and he was part of the history of the club. Rudy didn't talk much about his personal life, but people suspected he had some serious health problems. On June 27, 1968, Rudy sat despondent in a back room, holding a high-powered rifle. Moments later, at about 8:00 p.m., he shot himself in the chest and died in the hospital at 6:30 a.m. the next day. He told doctors that he had been contemplating suicide for several weeks because of his declining health.

As you might suspect, the back room where Rudy shot himself was the same room used by the owners as their office space. In a corner of the room, there was a chunk of plaster knocked out of the wall as if someone had hit the wall with a hammer. The hole in the wall looked bad, and it annoyed one of the owners. The hole turned out to be the bullet hole from Rudy's rifle on that fateful night.

Rudy was a restless spirit. Being a man of the Catholic faith, perhaps his spirit couldn't come to terms with his suicide. The ghostly phenomenon that occurred, according to a number of witnesses, was unnerving, disturbing and scary at times. Before long, encounters with Rudy became no laughing matter. The ghostly phenomena occurring inside the old Lake Club were downright amazing, and so many different people experienced them.

Both employees and customers would hear doors open and close on their own. Cold chills and inexplicable cool breezes would brush past in the bar area. Phantom music would suddenly fill the air, startling anyone hearing it. The owner's sons were once in a back room alone doing paperwork when they suddenly heard heavy footsteps in the hallway. Moments later, they heard someone strike the keys on a piano stored in the next room several times, getting their attention.

Rudy apparently had his own onstage presence. He would tamper with the controls on sound equipment. Instruments would curiously slip in and out of tune, making it difficult for entertainers to perform. Employees cleaning up at night heard a piano on the stage mysteriously play on its own, yet no one was near the piano. Sometimes it sounded like a child playfully slamming his fingers repeatedly on the keys. Another time, a trumpet sitting on the stage inexplicably sounded off with a volley of notes.

Musicians and performers had their own ghostly encounters with Rudy, oftentimes in the dressing rooms. Band members sometimes complained about sudden and sharp cold spots, phantom touches and a sense of not being alone. One time, two hairdryers turned on by themselves, causing the band members to hustle out of the room. A musician once went to the back storeroom, where the extra piano was stored, to check it out. As he entered the room, the piano suddenly started playing by itself, and a ghostly spectral hand appeared above the keys. Startled, the musician refused to go on stage that night, paranoid that his performance would be cursed.

The strange events that were occurring were getting more mysterious and bizarre. One bartender recalled setting down a shot glass on the bar, and before he could pour the drink into the glass, it suddenly flipped off the bar. The customer about fell off his barstool, and everyone around paused and looked at one another in disbelief. Glasses would occasionally slide down the bar and along the tables right in front of customers. Things were getting pretty freaky at the Sober Duck Disco. People were starting to become concerned for their safety, as the ghost seemed to be getting stronger and more aggressive with its antics.

One afternoon, a salesman stopped by to sell Tom something—a check writer perhaps. The two men sat at a table in the back office and went over the information. Suddenly, a glass lifted right off the table a couple of feet into the air, paused and then zipped across the room and smashed against the wall, breaking into pieces. Glass went everywhere. The spooked sales rep quickly scooted back in his chair and looked at Tom, as if to say, "Why did you throw the glass at me?" Of course, the salesman soon realized it wasn't Tom who had thrown the glass, and he nearly fell out of his chair trying to get away from the table. He stood up, turned and briskly walked out of the club. He never came back again.

Another time, Tom and Bill were in the office talking, and suddenly a water glass levitated right off the desk into the air and hovered over Bill for a moment. Then it turned over, dumping the water right into Bill's lap.

Though it was a little unnerving, both men had a good laugh, joking that Bill must have said something Rudy didn't approve of.

Tom was once bringing some extra chairs into the bar when he noticed a pile of dirty tablecloths on the floor. He picked them up and put them on the table. He went back for more chairs, and when he returned, the tablecloths were back on the floor. Again, he picked up the tablecloths and put them on the table, then went back for more chairs. When he returned, the tablecloths were back on the floor. Once again, he picked them up and put them on the table, but this time he waited and watched. Not a moment later, the tablecloths flew right off the table and onto the floor. Tom called out to Rudy, "Fine, just leave them on the floor!"

One very unnerving experience by one of the bartenders involved a face-to-face encounter with the ghostly apparition of Rudy. She was in a back bar area, the very back bar where Rudy had taken special customers, when all of a sudden a ghostly head appeared in the air above the bar and spoke to her. The mouth didn't move, but she could hear the voice tell her that one of the owners was going to die. She described the apparitional head as being pale, and she could see right through it. What stuck out for her was the hair: "It was snow white." She was so unsettled by the very bizarre encounter and the message that she kept it to herself, thinking one of the owners would, in fact, die if she said anything. But several weeks later, despite her silence, Harold Henderson, one of the original owners who still had ownership in the building, passed away.

One of Rudy's final pranks was a pretty good trick. A customer ordered a rum and coke. The waitress retrieved the drink from the bar and took it over to the customer. She set the drink down in front of him. Before she could leave the table, he immediately complained that his glass was full of chocolate. She looked at the drink, and it was, in fact, chocolate. The waitress had watched the bartender make the proper drink and had taken it right to the customer. There was no way for chocolate to get in the glass. Furthermore, at the time, there was no chocolate anywhere on the premises. But guess who liked chocolate?

Soon after that, Tom was at a class reunion and told a former classmate, who was now a priest, about the ghostly activity at the old club. He took an interest in the phenomena and agreed to come check it all out. The priest showed up with two other priests, and the three of them did a walk-through of the club area. Once in the back office, an eerie chill overcame the room, and one of the priests commented that there was one very restless soul in turmoil among them. He sensed that the spirit wanted to communicate

The back bar room, where Rudy would take his best customers for private drinks and cigars. This is also where a spectral Rudy appeared to a bartender and warned her of the impending death of one of the owners.

with them. All three priests agreed that it was not an evil presence, but a very restless soul indeed. An exorcism was not warranted, but offerings of prayer and blessings would be appropriate. The three priests began to walk through the entire club, reciting scripture, sprinkling holy water and offering blessings. Once in the back office room where Rudy had shot himself, they asked God for the repose of Rudy Cranor's soul and to receive him into heaven.

The ritual seemed to have worked. Things quieted down at the club; Rudy had finally crossed over. The owners said that Rudy Cranor had become part of their club family, even though no one was ever willing to stay late alone in the club. After the blessing, some of the staff commented that they kind of missed Rudy's antics, saying it was like having a practical joker around all the time. In the end, they all hoped Rudy was able to find peace.

But just like the original Lake Club, the nightclub business is a hard, fast and competitive world, and Tom and Bill decided to move on to other endeavors. New owners came along and tried other venues, but nothing could top or ever replace the old Lake Club.

The final chapter in the Lake Club history would unfold on an August morning in 1992. When firefighters arrived about 6:30 a.m., the building was already heavily involved in the fire, and by 8:00 a.m., the building was destroyed. It was arson, and the case remains unsolved to this day.

# SINISTER JOE NEVILLE

Community theater is an important part of cultural progress and development, and Springfield's Theater Guild was no exception. It was well supported by Springfield and had raised $175,000 for the construction of a new theater building. In 1951, the doors opened at its new theater on Lawrence Street. On opening night, November 6, all 482 seats were sold out for the performance of *Born Yesterday*.

Over the years, the community theater had been host to a number of well-known performances, such as *The Seven-Year Itch*, *Anastasia*, *Oklahoma* and even *Our American Cousin*, made famous by Lincoln's assassination. Performances generally received positive reviews, and the guild boasted membership of approximately three thousand.

Today, the curtain is down, the seats are empty and the doors are locked. The stage at the old theater is silent. The theater has had its last curtain call, and it is now for sale.

The theater is believed to be one of the more haunted places in Springfield. Theater-type people, like sports players, can be quite superstitious. Since 1955, some thespians believe that every performance at the community theater was cursed and plagued by problems, glitches and mishaps. There is a dark and sometimes malevolent presence that has a hold on this old theater. It has been known to make its presence felt by any unsuspecting visitor violating its domain.

Locations where intense emotions have been imprinted on the environment, such as old theaters, are conducive to ghostly activity. Actors

The Springfield Theater Center, where the malevolent spirit of Joe Neville guards his territory.

and audience alike express a wide range of emotions during performances. There's laughter and sadness, anger and fear, love and hate, and over time, it is believed that this energy somehow stays with the theater long after the curtains close. Plays often tell the story of some tragedy, yet it would be a real-life tragic event that would set the stage for the theater haunting of sinister Joe Neville.

The haunted history unfolded on the night of May 13, 1955, when an actor named Joe Neville left the theater after rehearsal, went home and committed suicide.

It turned out that the company that Joe had worked for had done an audit, and Joe had been fingered by the auditor for a substantial amount of money that had been unaccounted for. Unable to face the humiliation of the charge, Joe took the easy way out.

Joe was known by his peers to be a bit of an eccentric and temperamental guy, and he always seemed to have a smoke lit. Joe was not very friendly with most folks. He was a difficult man of arrogant disposition. But the theater soothed Joe's temperament, and he was clearly tamed when on stage.

Joe was said to be a decent actor, and his colleagues tolerated his volatile temperament. His peers also tolerated the strong smell of Noxzema that surrounded Joe. He had a persistent rash on his legs, and it is believed that he used the cream as a treatment.

Joe's past was, however, shrouded in mystery. It was rumored that he had acted and directed plays in England, but under a different name. When he left England to come to the United States, Joe gave away a lot of land to various people—but the thing is, Joe didn't own any of the land he gave away.

At the time of Joe's death, he was for the first time playing the lead role in an upcoming performance, realizing his ambition. But Joe was dead, and he was replaced. The show must go on.

Some believe Joe was upset that the show went on without him. Some believe Joe and his temperamental disposition returned to the theater to vent his frustrations on all future performances.

At first, strange and bizarre—yet harmless—things occurred, like lights flickering or turning on and off. Things became inexplicable—doors would open and close on their own and strange noises or unintelligible voices could be heard. Props sailed through the air across the stage right in front of actors; other times, props were moved about and were not in place when actors reached for them.

Over time, the hauntings escalated. During play rehearsals, a dark shadowy figure lurking amongst the seats distracted performers on stage. Some actors claimed to see a faint orange glow where the dark figure was sitting, convincing them that it was Joe smoking a cigarette. Other times, the dark shadow was seen on the catwalk above the stage during performances, when no one was supposed to be up there. Actors were distracted by a presence felt on stage. Though no one was seen, some actors were convinced they were not standing there alone, especially when pushed by unseen hands. Actors and stage hands claimed to have seen the actual apparition of Joe standing just off stage. They became superstitious that if they saw Joe, their performance would be cursed and receive poor reviews.

Actors at times have to make costume changes during shows. On several known occasions, actors stepped off stage to make a very fast costume change, only to find their costumes missing. Costumes were later found neatly folded under a stairwell; another time, the costumes were found strewn over a ladder away from the stage. Other times, props put into place prior to performances would disappear from stage when actors reached for them.

The fact that strange things would happen during performances only served to unravel the nerves of some actors. Some actors became more concerned about Joe playing pranks during shows than trying to remember their lines. One of the most known onstage pranks that occurred during a performance happened when an actor answered a telephone call as part of the show. When he picked up the phone, which was obviously not hooked up to a phone line, to act out the phone call, he heard static through the receiver. Speechless, the actor paused in astonishment. The actor next to him quietly muttered his next line to him, but he remained shocked, and it took several more seconds for him to recover from the awkward moment. The performance ended without further incident, but the actor became fearful, thinking that Joe had targeted his performance.

With each bizarre event, the more the actors talked about Joe, the more superstitious they became. Superstition gave into fear, and Joe seemed to feed off the fear. The hauntings became more pronounced and frightful. Believers of Joe's presence were convinced that the naysayers only angered Joe's restless spirit.

Then, Joe's angry spirit became downright dangerous. He began to actually attack people.

On one known occasion, a crew was busy building a stage set and discussing the existence of Joe. During a smoke break on stage, one of the guys voiced his doubts that Joe was real and claimed that there was no such thing as ghosts. All of a sudden, without warning, a nearby circular saw started up on its own. Several sheets of plywood fell over, crashing to the floor, followed by a tall stepladder to the side of the stage. One of the guys claimed that he half expected Joe's ghost to actually appear. Needless to say, the carpenters were done working for the night.

But as the years passed, so did the intensity of the hauntings. Performances continued to be belabored by petty occurrences—perhaps due to poor stage-managing, or perhaps Joe is still lingering, seeking the attention for a performance he never gave.

Though Joe had seemingly moved on, the occasional distinct and pungent smell of Noxzema wafting through the theater air would alert people of his continued presence. The use of the cream in the theater was banned years ago, ever since Joe's death.

But the story doesn't exactly end there.

In the 1990s, the theater center on Lawrence Street closed its doors and moved the organization to the newly constructed Hoogland Theater for the Arts, a modern theater building with three separate auditoriums. With the community theater group now functioning here, the shows go on to this day, and the stories of sinister old Joe Neville still linger in the minds of some of the veteran actors. Old superstitions die hard; some actors believe Joe has followed the group to its new location. During rehearsals, some actors have been unnerved by the presence of a dark, shadowy figure sitting amongst the seats in the back of the auditorium. Too hard to believe, you say? Then explain the faint orange glow of a lit cigarette accompanying the shadow man. Still, it's the faint smell of Noxzema in the air that unnerves actors even today.

# SPRINGFIELD'S HAUNTED CASTLE

George Brinkerhoff came to Springfield after graduating from Gettysburg College well before the famous Civil War battle. He became a member of the Illinois bar, and he used his law education to further his various business ventures in insurance and farm loans. He had a short friendship with Abraham Lincoln, but he had left an impression on Mary Lincoln, who asked Mr. Brinkerhoff to serve as an honorary pallbearer at Lincoln's Springfield funeral.

Using his wealth, he had a beautiful Victorian Italianate mansion built in 1869, which became known as the "Castle." George and his wife, Isabella, along with their six children, lived in the home. The home cost about $25,000 to build at the time, and it served not only as a residence and place of entertainment but also as a testament to the success of George Brinkerhoff. The property was originally several acres in size, and Brinkerhoff's favorite pastime was horticulture. He constructed a large greenhouse southeast of the home. His greenhouse supplied local florists for years. There was also a small dairy once located on the property.

For almost thirty years, the Brinkerhoff home thrived and prospered, despite the death of one of their infant children in the home. The home was host to a great number of dinner parties and social events that were well attended. Upon the death of Isabella in 1894, George held fewer social events at the castle, but he still managed to run his greenhouse and other businesses until his death in 1928.

Mr. Brinkerhoff left his home to the Ursuline Convent upon his death. Since 1929, the old Brinkerhoff home had many uses, such as classrooms

Springfield's haunted "Castle," the Brinkerhoff home.

and dorm rooms for a junior college. The basement was once used by the Springfield Theater Guild as its first theater home. Today, the home has been restored, and the social events have returned. The home can be rented out for receptions, parties and other activities. Ghosts are included with the rental price. It seems George Brinkerhoff and some others may still be in the castle, not only looking after the home but also playing pranks and socializing with the contemporary guests.

A number of ghostly encounters have been quietly talked about for years. It seems the most active spirit in the house is quite the prankster and likes to play attention-getting pranks on various people in the home. Strange things occur all over the home at all hours of the day and night.

George Brinkerhoff died in his second-floor bedroom, and most believe that it's his spirit that haunts and plays pranks in the house. His ghostly and benevolent specter has been seen throughout the house from time to time. An instructor once opened George's old bedroom door, now an office, only to be startled by the faint, blurry figure of a man in nineteenth-century clothing who quickly disappeared right in front of her eyes. It happened so fast that she wasn't sure it was nothing more than her overactive imagination. Yet other workers and guests have reported seeing the figure of a man passing by a distant doorway or crossing a hall. Each encounter seems to last only for a split second. George is thought to play his pranks in the library, where he apparently likes to move around books and other objects—sometimes right before the eyes of unwitting witnesses. One guest in the house once reported sitting and reading a particular book when she was called away to take a phone call. When she returned to the empty library minutes later, the book she had been reading had been re-shelved, to her amazement. She had heard of George's antics and called out "Good one!" to him. The light from a nearby floor lamp momentarily flickered.

People working in the home over the years have reported hearing the phantom sound of a baby or young child crying. The sound seems to come from the upper floors, but anyone trying to track the sound through the house to find the crying child is always unable to discern exactly where the crying is coming from. Any efforts to call out and comfort the crying child only result in immediate silence. The faint sound can be unnerving to some—especially mothers—and some people believe it is the sound of the Brinkerhoff child who died in infancy. But the ghostly pitter-patter of children's feet and giggling have also been heard throughout various parts of the house.

Other ghostly things occur in the house, as you might expect, such as lights flickering for no known reason and the sound of doors opening and closing on their own. One staff member spoke about working at her desk and sensing that someone was there watching her, though she could see no one present. She said one day she even called out to the spirit to stop watching her. Though the sensation went away, it still would occasionally return. Perhaps it's George Brinkerhoff himself. Office workers in the house talk about electronics and computers turning on or off seemingly by themselves. One secretary spoke about occasionally hearing the keys on a computer keyboard clicking away as if someone were typing away, but no hands were seen. She claims the phantom typist no longer unnerves her and is now just good company, especially on rainy days.

Today, the home is host to receptions and various social events that are not immune to the ghostly happenings. Deejays and other entertainers sometimes complain of difficulty getting certain electronics to work properly, and then suddenly the machines will work fine moments later without any plausible explanation. Photographers at receptions have had difficulty getting their cameras to work properly at times. Cameras sometimes are inexplicably unable to focus on the subject and have been known to suddenly drain of battery power. It's even said that caterers have had trouble with appetizers on trays getting moved about, messing up food counts (though this could simply be a really hungry server blaming the missing food on George).

But not all the ghostly activity occurs inside the old Brinkerhoff home. Next to one of the old academic buildings is a small parking lot that was once a small cemetery for the sisters of the convent. But a city ordinance in 1876 required that all cemeteries in the city be moved outside the city limits. This ordinance not only affected the convent's cemetery, but you may also recall that it forced the removal of the old Hutchinson Cemetery, where Springfield High School is now located. The graves at the convent were moved to the Calvary Cemetery, next to the Oak Ridge Cemetery. This old parking lot is now the site of a number of ghostly incidents. Students and teachers alike have had unnerving encounters with phantom specters lurking in the shadows and dark shadowy figures inexplicably drifting though the area. Staff members parking in the lot are sometimes unnerved walking to their cars, hoping not to see any dark figures in the vicinity. In fact, the dark and ghostly figures have been seen wandering through various parts of the campus at random. Though the figures may be frightening to some, most believe the ghostly figures are the spirits of sisters who have crossed over into the light but have returned to watch over the convent where they spent many years of their lives. The school and convent were a place where these sisters not only provided others with an education but also developed in them a strong Christian faith and taught them to worship God.

I'd like to think the spirits are crossed-over sisters and earthbound angels who have returned to the campus and Brinkerhoff home to watch over matters and to guide the younger sisters and students in their spiritual development. But I can't help wondering if the ghostly sisters of the convent remain to admonish old George Brinkerhoff for his boyish pranks in the castle that Brinkerhoff built.

# About the Author

G arret Moffett is the author of *Haunted Macomb* with The History Press and has been the owner and operator of Springfield Walks since 2006.

Visit us at
www.historypress.net